Managing Change
to Reduce Resistance

The Results–Driven Manager Series

The Results–Driven Manager Series collects timely articles from *Harvard Management Update and Harvard Management Communication Letter* to help senior to middle managers sharpen their skills, increase their effectiveness, and gain a competitive edge. Presented in a concise, accessible format to save managers valuable time, these books offer authoritative insights and techniques for improving job performance and achieving immediate results.

Other books in the series:

Teams That Click

Presentations That Persuade and Motivate

Face-to-Face Communications for Clarity and Impact

Winning Negotiations That Preserve Relationships

Managing Yourself for the Career You Want

Getting People on Board

Taking Control of Your Time

Dealing with Difficult People

Becoming an Effective Leader

Motivating People for Improved Performance

A Timesaving Guide

THE RESULTS-DRIVEN MANAGER

RDM

Managing Change
to Reduce
Resistance

• • •

Harvard Business School Press

Boston, Massachusetts

Copyright 2005 Harvard Business School Publishing Corporation
All rights reserved.
Printed in the United States of America
09 08 07 06 05   5 4 3 2 1

Library of Congress Cataloging-in-Publication Data

The results-driven manager : managing change to reduce resistance.
        p.   cm. — (The results-driven manager series)
      ISBN 1-59139-781-2
    1. Organizational change—Management.   I. Title: Managing
change to reduce resistance. II. Harvard Business School Press.
III. Series.
      HD58.8.R4935 2005
      658.4'063—dc22
                              2005001315

The paper used in this publication meets the requirements of the
American National Standard for Permanence of Paper for Publications
and Documents in Libraries and Archives Z39.48-1992.

Contents

3-1-06

Contents

Managing Change
to Reduce Resistance

Introduction

. . .

Like a living organism, your company operates within a constantly changing environment. New business realities—in the form of unexpected technologies, emerging markets, and radical innovations that rewrite the rules of competition—continually present fresh challenges. To survive and stay ahead of rivals, your company must adapt to those new realities quickly—and that requires you and other managers to drive change effectively.

Many organizations strive for adaptability by defining new competitive strategies based on their analysis of what they see happening in their industry. For example, a company might set out to become the lowest-cost provider in a particular market, develop offerings that feature the most cutting-edge technologies, or satisfy a unique consumer need that no other firm has identified yet. Different parts of the company—research and development, marketing, human resources, and other

1

functions—then carry out change initiatives designed to support the corporate strategy.

As a manager, you can—and must—help your organization seize advantage of new business realities by driving change in your team, department, or division. By leading change successfully, you generate valuable results for your company. You strengthen your organization's ability to respond quickly to new business conditions with creative, innovative products and services. You help your company establish efficient processes that enable it to stay one step ahead of change. And you contribute to its ability to compete and to profit from change.

A Daunting Challenge

But as you may have surmised based on your own experiences as a manager, driving change isn't easy. Perhaps you've discovered that many employees find change painful—especially when it entails large-scale shifts in the way they do their work. Such individuals may have mounted intense resistance to a change initiative you've presented. Or maybe you've sensed that your direct reports have exhausted themselves trying to keep up with the ever-accelerating pace of change that characterizes business today. Your people may have become so "burned out" on change that they view every new initiative as just another management fad imposed by out-of-touch bosses.

Of course, with the business landscape shifting in ever more dramatic ways, your company must do more than just respond to current customer needs and competitive pressures. Instead, it has to "look beyond its headlights" to anticipate changes that are farther and farther ahead in the road. That makes driving change even more difficult.

Perhaps you've found that the biggest challenge to change comes with success: Even if your company is doing well, it still needs to anticipate and prepare responses to new challenges that have barely made themselves visible over the horizon. Otherwise, it will be caught flat-footed when those challenges gather momentum and suddenly appear on the company's doorstep. However, your people have responded to your call for change with "Why *should* we change? We're doing fine!"

All of these challenges to driving change are so daunting that, perhaps not surprisingly, two out of three change initiatives fail. Yes, this statistic is sobering. It may even have you thinking, "If that many change efforts don't pan out, what is the likelihood that I can lead change successfully in *my* company?" But you *can* boost your chances of beating the odds—if you apply fundamental change-leadership strategies, understand and combat the major obstacles to change (including complacency), and communicate effectively about change in your group or unit.

The articles in this volume address each of these change-leadership areas. Here's a preview of what you'll find as you read this book.

Applying Fundamental Change-Leadership Strategies

Though changing an organization is a complex challenge, some companies and departments do succeed in reinventing themselves frequently and quickly in the face of constantly shifting business conditions. Even more impressive, they sustain and even enhance this ability to adapt. How can you help ensure that *your* company beats the change-leadership odds? Identify and apply the fundamental change strategies that drive success in leading companies. The articles in this section describe some of the more striking strategies and explain how you can apply them.

In the first article—"Creating the Climate for Change: Mobilizing the Executive Team and Your Organization"— business writer Katherine Kane describes a potent change-leadership process comprising four steps: (1) *Signal change with evocative symbols.* An executive at one retailer handed out rulers to store managers to launch a change initiative that required managers to ask customers about their buying preferences when the managers were standing within ten feet of customers in a store. (2) *Enlist constituents.* Explain the reason for a needed change effort from the point of view of those you're leading. For example, point out how your direct reports will benefit from the change, and honestly assess the difficult aspects of the change. (3) *Align your department.* Ensure that the actions you're asking your people to take directly support the new direction your company has defined. (4) *Face resistance.* Put resisters in a position in which they can feel the impact of failing to change. One police commissioner required constituents to ride the New York subway system for thirty days to see firsthand the extent of the crime problem he had determined to solve through a specific change initiative.

In "Short-Term Wins—The Linchpin of a Change Initiative," you'll learn how to apply another powerful change-leadership technique: scoring small successes early in a change effort to create and sustain momentum for larger change. By helping your people achieve short-term wins, you enable them to see that change *is* possible—and worthwhile. You also strengthen the organizational capabilities essential for sustainable high performance in the long run. The authors provide several suggestions for generating short-term wins. For example, break complex tasks down into components, then tackle the simpler components first. Focus ruthlessly on solving the concrete business problems embedded in the smaller change projects you've identified. And communicate a sense of urgency to keep your employees focused on the tasks at hand.

In the next article—"How to Get Aboard a Major Change Effort"—management guru John Kotter emphasizes the value of managers modeling change-readiness for their employees. According to Kotter, too many managers respond to an announced change initiative by either giving in to pessimism or assuming that change will be easy and quick. If this describes you, begin modeling change-readiness by accepting that change is essential *and* difficult. Open yourself to learning more about change in order to lead it in your group. Also clarify the vision behind the initiative—by talking with your own supervisor—so you can communicate that vision to your people and ensure that everyone is striving toward the same goal. And, to combat cynicism among employees regarding change, marshal evidence from your company's top ranks that this newest effort is going to be different—that it's going to put the organization in a far better position that its current performance allows.

Tom Krattenmaker, director of news and information at Swarthmore College, builds further on the idea of combating cynicism in his article "Change Through Appreciative Inquiry." Through the appreciative inquiry process, you can help your employees focus on possibilities rather than problems to define needed change and develop a plan for achieving it. To encourage appreciative inquiry, invite your employees to come together to talk not about problems and solutions, but about their greatest successes. Have them describe what their department or team is like when it is at its best. Then ask them to identify common themes in the resulting stories. Invite them to conceive a vision of what their group might achieve in the brightest possible future. Finally, working backward from that vision, help them define the steps and resources that will enable them to realize it. "The way people talk about their organizations shapes their behavior within them," Krattenmaker writes. Appreciative inquiry creates a tremendous positive energy that organizations can then channel into executing change.

In the last two articles in this section, strategy-implementation experts Robert S. Kaplan and David P. Norton of the Balanced Scorecard Collaborative maintain that unless managers can carry out the changes needed to create value for their organizations, the company's overall strategy is useless. To implement those changes, managers must invest in four forms of "organization capital": *culture, leadership, alignment,* and *teamwork.* Part I of this two-part series, "Organization Capital: Supporting the Change Agenda That Supports Strategy Execution," focuses on the *cultural* component. According to Kaplan and Norton, you can help build a change-ready culture in your group or unit by ensuring that all your employees are aware of and internalize the mission, vision, and core values needed to execute the company's strategy. The authors suggest identifying cultural characteristics needed to support the strategy—for example, "customer focus," "continuous improvement," "risk taking," or "teamwork"—and measuring current cultural values through employee surveys. They also point out that different parts of an organization may need different cultures in order to best support the corporate strategy. Accordingly, ask yourself what kind of culture *your* department or team needs to help execute the organization's strategy.

Part II of the series, "Organization Capital: Leadership, Alignment, and Teamwork," introduces the remaining three forms of organization capital. As with culture, Kaplan and Norton offer recommendations specific to each of these forms. For example, regarding *leadership*, you need to model the attitudes and behaviors you expect your direct reports to display. For *alignment*, you help employees understand how their personal roles support the overall strategy. And for *teamwork* (which the authors also call knowledge sharing), you motivate people to document their ideas and knowledge. When you strengthen teamwork, you enable employees in other parts of the organization to readily access the knowledge and use it to make improvements in their own functions.

Addressing Major Obstacles to Change

In addition to applying potent change-leadership strategies, you also need to familiarize yourself with—and remove—the more common major obstacles to change.

These obstacles require specialized approaches tailored particularly to the change effort in question. The articles in this section describe these obstacles and explain how to remove them.

Business writer Lauren Keller Johnson starts things off with "Debriefing Eric Abrahamson: The Road to Better Recombination." As Abrahamson explains in this interview-based article, one of the biggest obstacles to successful change efforts is a tendency among managers and executives to force *too* much change at once. By going overboard with change, you "trigger excruciating cycles of initiative overload, chaos, and employee burnout. To reverse these cycles, . . . we must change how we change." Instead of the usual "creative destruction," Abrahamson recommends reconfiguring and adapting your company's existing assets—people, structures, culture, processes, and networks—to achieve "faster, cheaper, painless, and sustainable transformation." For example, when Westland Helicopters was suffering from change overload, managers adapted an effective product-development model from the company's in-house software division for use in helicopter production, minimizing product-design costs. They also borrowed a product proposition that another division had long used to build a highly successful customizable helicopter.

In "How to Overcome 'Change Fatigue,'" business writer Nick Morgan takes a closer look at ways to combat the exhaustion employees experience at companies in which executives impose large-scale change from the top. To avoid change fatigue in your team or department, encourage "bottom-up" initiation of change. Morgan shares an example: At the Brazilian manufacturing firm Semco, "employees select their jobs, titles, places and hours of work, and even pay." Managers conduct twice-yearly 360-degree performance evaluations to identify needed changes. Leaders are picked by their subordinates. And since almost all leaders "come from within the company, no radical changes are imposed by new leaders from the outside trying to make a good impression." Moreover, "the CEO's position changes continually: four people regularly rotate through the job every year." In short, at Semco change is the responsibility of groups of employees, not senior leaders. Employees thus feel a strong sense of ownership of change—which counteracts feelings of fatigue.

In "So They Do More Than Survive," consultant Sharon Drew Morgen switches focus from change fatigue to fear of and resistance to change—additional major obstacles to a successful change effort. How to help your employees move past fear and resistance and emerge better off after a change effort? Morgen recommends using questions to address the uncertainty that accompanies change. For example, ask your employees how they see the current change affecting them and their job environment, and what they need from you to help carry out the needed transformation. Ask what skills they must acquire or strengthen and how they might recognize warning signs that the change is creating crisis in their work environment. By posing such questions and discussing the responses collectively with your team, you ensure that each person is seen, heard, and taken into account. As Morgen notes, "By bringing everyone into the equation, the odds are good that the change will be for the better."

As another major obstacle to change, your company needs to strike a delicate balance: improving profitability while also building employees' capacity to solve new, continually arising challenges. The next article in this section—"How Does Change Management Need to Change?"—examines this theme. Harvard Business School professors Michael Beer and Nitin Nohria use the terms "Theory E" (change needed to improve economic value) and "Theory O" (change needed to enhance organizational capacities) to describe the two horns of this dilemma. Each type of change has its advantages. For example, theory E change leaders can generate quick financial results, while theory O leaders can establish long-term adaptability throughout the organization. Rather than focusing exclusively on one or the other type of change, you need to combine the best of both to lead successful change.

The final article in this section addresses a challenge facing more and more managers today: how to anticipate and implement needed change long before the need for change reaches the crisis point. In "The Change Audit: A New Tool to Monitor Your Biggest Organizational Challenge," business writer Lila Booth proposes conducting a *change audit* to strengthen your department's or team's ability to anticipate and prepare for long-term transformation. You conduct a change audit before, during, and after each change initiative. For example, before the change, analyze the history of response to change in your group or department, identifying patterns that you want to avoid during the upcoming change. During the change, assess the stresses that the process has created and create a time line for implementation and a set of performance measures. And after the change, ask, "What did we do well and not do well?" and "What next?"

Driving Change Without a "Burning Platform"

Of all the obstacles to successful change, high performance within your organization or department can prove the most dangerous. Without a "burning platform" to create a sense of urgency around change, your employees may ask why they should bother to revise the way they work. After all, the company, division, or team is doing well, and there's no crisis in sight. But managers who wait for a crisis to jump-start change risk seeing their team or division caught flat-footed when the crisis hits. The articles in this section provide suggestions for driving change if your organization or unit lacks a burning platform.

In "Is Your Company a Prisoner of Its Own Success?" business writer Loren Gary describes numerous techniques you can use to combat change resistance if your unit or company is doing well. For example, to overcome complacency, create new structures that enable your employees to strengthen their change-readiness. Managers at one company reworked the firm's product-development process into "cross-functional teams that would assemble and develop a new product, collaborate for the duration of a project, and then disband." They also "bought new furniture with wheels so that employees could roll their desks and files from one team to another." These new structures encouraged flexibility and adaptability—qualities essential for continual change-readiness even in the absence of an immediate need for change.

In "Debriefing Richard Koppel: Change Without a Burning Platform," Lauren Keller Johnson describes how the vice president of research and development at GTECH Corporation, a lottery network firm, drove change despite lack of an immediate crisis. Realizing that the highly successful company would eventually be left behind if it didn't start using newer Web-based technologies, Koppel nevertheless encountered stiff resistance to the idea from in-house engineers. To overcome that resistance, he applied five principles that any manager can put into practice: (1) constantly make the business case for change; (2) demonstrate that you're committed to making the change happen—even if it means letting some change resisters go; (3) dictate the desired outcome, but let your employees determine how to reach that goal; (4) admit your mistakes; and (5) explain in specific terms the consequences of not making the required changes.

The final article in this section—business writer Betty A. Marton's "If It Ain't Broke, Fix It Anyway: Communicating to Create Change at Ford"—offers another company example of how to drive change without a burning platform. At the time Ford launched a large-scale change initiative involving streamlining and unifying its worldwide operations, business overall was brisk. But "projected trends showed an inevitable competitive decline—unless the company did something drastically different." Managers in Ford's communication services department played a vital role in getting the message out about the importance of the change effort. "The company's in-house communication team," Marton writes, "produced an ongoing avalanche of print, video, and electronic media that gave employees the information they needed—both good and bad—consistently, frequently, and before they heard it from outside sources."

Ford's managers also encouraged "uphill" and "downhill" communication. For example, senior managers exchanged information cross-functionally with other employees. They also developed techniques for delivering consistent messages about change to employees in countries around the world where Ford had manufacturing sites. These efforts paid big dividends—in the form of reduced costs as well as increased productivity, profits, shareholder value, and market capitalization.

Communicating Effectively
About Change

As the Ford story suggests, effective communication is a key tool for managers seeking to drive successful change. How to strengthen your communication skills and get the message out to your employees about the importance of change? The ideas in this section's articles provide valuable guidelines.

In "Communicating Change: A Dozen Tips from the Experts," business writer Rebecca M. Saunders distills twelve change-communication strategies from top change theorists. Here are some of these strategies in brief: (1) specify what the change is expected to achieve; (2) explain the business reasons behind corporate changes; (3) let your employees know the scope of the change; (4) frequently repeat the purpose of the change and the actions planned; (5) use graphics to simplify corporate restructures.

Harvard Business School Publishing newsletter editor Angelia Herrin examines change communication from a different angle in "You're Ready for Top-Line Growth— Are Your Employees?" In this article, Herrin stresses the importance of using different communication strategies at different stages of a change effort. For instance, when you're first introducing the idea that change is needed in your unit or organization, "sell the problem." Talk in "every forum possible about the reasons for change and the cost of not addressing the problem." Later, when your team or unit is in "the halfway time between the old way of doing things and the new," show that you are personally willing to try some risks. When your unit or organization has transitioned to a "new beginning," ensure that your words and actions match up. For example, "don't preach teamwork and then publicly praise individual contribution."

In "Debriefing Howard Gardner: Tactics for Changing Minds," Lauren Keller Johnson presents helpful suggestions from Gardner, a professor at Harvard University's school of education. According to Gardner, you get the best results by communicating the desired vision behind a change effort in multiple formats. These formats include stories, numerical information, pictures, charts, metaphors, and analogies. What's the advantage of using multiple formats? By depicting the proposed vision in different ways, you increase the chances that your employees will understand your idea—which is an essential first step to driving change.

The final selection, consultant Stever Robbins's "Communication as a Change Tool," shines the spotlight on the theme of stories as a powerful tool for communicating about change. A compelling story, Robbins explains, can help motivate employees to enact change and to envision your unit's or organization's long-term future. The most effective stories "make information visible" to employees. For instance, one purchasing manager who had tried unsuccessfully to cut costs "quietly assembled an exhibit of work gloves, all purchased at wildly different prices from different vendors by his managers around the country. He piled the gloves on a table—revealing a lot of duplication—and invited his managers in for a visit. They quickly understood the problem."

Though driving change is difficult for any manager, you can boost your chances of success by applying the guidelines described in this collection. As you read, keep the following questions in mind:

- What are the two or three fundamental change-leadership strategies that will most help me drive change in my unit or company?

- What are the biggest obstacles to driving change in my unit or company? What techniques can I develop to remove those obstacles?

- If my company is currently very successful, how can I impress upon people the importance of being change-ready so that we sustain that success?

- How do I usually communicate about change with my direct reports? In what ways can I make my communications more effective?

Applying Fundamental Change-Leadership Strategies

• • •

The most successful change leaders apply fundamental strategies to help their companies reinvent themselves quickly in the face of ever-accelerating change. The articles in this section show you how to use these same strategies to achieve equally impressive results in *your* company.

For example, you'll discover the power of using short-term wins to create and sustain momentum for larger change efforts, and learn how to model change-readiness for your employees. You'll also find out how to help your team or unit define a compelling vision—and a plan for achieving it—by asking what's possible, not what's problematic. And you'll learn to use a potent methodology, the Balanced Scorecard, to establish the right culture and teamwork to win support for change in your unit or company.

Creating the Climate for Change

Mobilizing the Executive Team and Your Organization

· · ·

Katherine Kane

Managing change is fundamentally a people issue. It's about motivation and influencing behavior, about breaking old habits and attitudes, and about creating an environment that's conducive to embracing the new. According to Jay Conger, one of the world's preeminent authorities on leadership and corporate governance, the most critical ingredient in any change effort is leadership. Surprisingly, though, surveys show that most employees do not consider their top executives to be very effective at driving organizational change. Conger has crystallized his approach to leading change into four dimensions, all of which, he counsels, should be used in the early stages of implementation.

Jay Conger has seen the challenges of leadership up close and personal. A researcher at the Center for Effective Organizations at the University of Southern California and author or coauthor of several books, including *Growing Your Company's Leaders: How Great Organizations Use Succession Management to Sustain Competitive Advantage, Corporate Boards: New Strategies for Adding Value at the Top,* and *Winning 'Em Over: A New Model for Managing in the Age of Persuasion,* Conger has studied a variety of organizations from Dow Chemical to Toyota. Leadership, Conger believes, is the most essential foundation for successfully creating change. Yet surveys show that most employees do not find their CEO or senior executive team effective in driving consistent change throughout the organization.

Effective leaders acknowledge and address the challenges of change in their organization. They are also aware that leading a change effort can be dangerous; as Machiavelli's *The Prince* illustrates, leaders of change leave behind them a host of enemies from the old guard and enjoy only the lukewarm support of the others. Conger supports an approach to leading change based on four dimensions: signaling (and signifying) change, enlisting constituents, aligning the organization, and facing resistance. These concepts run parallel to the principles embedded in the Balanced Scorecard and the Strategy-Focused Organization (mobilize, translate, align, motivate, and govern). Conger believes that these phases are not necessarily exclusive and distinct but should all be considered comprehensively in the early stage of implementation. But he warns that leading a change effort is no easy task.

Bringing about change is easier said than done, Conger explains, because by our nature, human beings resist the unknown and the unfamiliar. We are comfortable with the status quo, no matter how many problems lie underneath. Good leaders shake things up; they reveal the deeper problems often hidden by successes. They make more work for us on the road to less work. And, because it is virtually impossible for even the best leaders to anticipate all of the obstacles along the way, there will always be unexpected roadblocks. Flexibility is the key to navigating the path of change.

The Encyclopaedia Britannica Company's near demise serves as a textbook example of the consequences of executives' failure to recognize the magnitude of impending change—and respond quickly. An industry leader for more than two centuries, Encyclopaedia Britannica Company was faced with a technological revolution that would turn the industry on its head. With the advent of the CD-ROM in the 1980s, company executives grappled with whether and how far to adopt the new technology. They feared that the cheap CD-ROM format would cannibalize their traditional multivolume product (which today costs around $1,400). Though the

> Gone are the command-and-control days of executives managing by decree. Acquiring missionaries is a powerful way to expand the reach of a change program and ensure its duration.

company had already shown itself to be an innovator in electronic publishing by making *Britannica* the first encyclopedia available online (through Lexus Nexus) in 1981 and by releasing its *Compton's MultiMedia Encyclopedia* in CD-ROM in the late 1980s, it did not issue its flagship encyclopedia on CD-ROM until 1994, after Microsoft's Encarta had already been on the market. At the time, executives never considered the $50 Encarta, derived from *Funk & Wagnalls Encyclopedia,* its competition; what they didn't realize was that their competition was, in fact, the computer. As executives continued to debate the appropriate marketing strategy for transitioning from the direct sale of the hardbound edition to a mix of electronic and print products, *Britannica* lost precious market share. Despite executives' recognition of the technological change, their inability to adapt rapidly to it ultimately cost them. Within five years, Microsoft was the number one seller of encyclopedias, and Encyclopaedia Britannica Company was struggling to survive.

More often than not, Conger observes, the future is already here—it's just a matter of recognizing it. Encyclopaedia Britannica was historically a sales company, and some executives could not comprehend selling CD-ROMs at a much lower price than one of their beautiful hard-cover volumes. The threat of innovation and an overall change in corporate strategy was too much for executives to face. Conger recalls something Peter Drucker once said: "The art of leadership is the art of abandonment." Effective change agents know when to let go of the old ways of doing business and forge ahead with the new.

Signal—and Signify—Change

To create a change-friendly climate, executives must first signal change by creating significant moments. By actually staging an event or story that resonates with the masses, change agents have a greater opportunity to challenge the old system and brand their new initiative. Asda is one example of a company that knew how to create a significant moment to bring about change in its corporate culture. This U.K. retail chain (similar to a Sam's Club in the U.S. and part of the Wal-Mart group)

25

historically required store managers to wear jackets on the shop floor. One change agent knew that this practice actually made managers less approachable to customers. He gathered all the company's managers in a group setting and made them all take their jackets off. Then, he gave each of them a coat hanger that read "No Jacket Required." He also gave them each a ruler and explained a new rule—the "10-Foot Rule"—which mandated that any time a manager was within 10 feet of a customer, he or she would be required to approach that customer and try to understand that customer's buying preferences. This change in management and shift in strategy—cultural changes brought on by internal rules—turned the company around. By being given coat hangers and a ruler, managers had symbols to remind them of the new way of operating.

Enlist Constituents

Conger warns that if there ever were a time for business-people to learn the fine art of persuasion, it is now. Gone are the command-and-control days of executives managing by decree. Today businesses are run largely by cross-functional teams of peers and populated by baby boomers and their Generation X offspring, who show little tolerance for unquestioned authority. Acquiring missionaries is a powerful way to expand the reach of a change program and ensure its duration. Conger suggests enlisting constituents or attracting people to a common purpose.

Conger believes that getting buy-in from constituents is best accomplished through "micro-leading"—that is, leading from the bottom up. Leaders must set an example though their own actions—taking on their most important performance challenges to achieve a strategy and doing the frontline work from which they are typically removed. This could include fielding customer complaints or directly providing service to clients. Next, it is critical to provide a story around where the organization is headed and why. And to enlist support, it is important to explain change from the point of view of those being led, not from the point of view of the top echelon. Engineers may not understand or care about the same issues that the shareholders do. Change agents need missionaries, and missionaries need a relevant story to relate to. Leaders must be honest with these missionaries about what the change will cost them and what is in it for them in the long run. What are the consequences of not acting? How will the change be rolled out? What tools and resources are available to make the change easier? These issues must be addressed if the staff in any organization is to buy into the new idea.

Align the Organization

As leaders attempt to mobilize their employees toward change, it is essential to align the entire organization, from the board of directors all the way down to those responsible for the basic support functions. Leaders use simple and memorable rules of alignment, which are called the "must-do's." The best leaders use these rules to align the organization strategically and tactically. For example, Jack Welch of GE came up with a memorable but simple strategic "must-do": to be number one or number two in every industry in which the company had operations. A tactical "must-do" is illustrated by the Ritz-Carlton hotel's guideline for associates at the front desk: "Answer the phone by the third ring, with a smile." With a vision and aligning "must-do's" in place, change agents then need to back them up with methodologies for each new initiative, such as the Six Sigma process improvement approach. Choosing individual champions rather than committees for discrete new projects enables staff to feel a sense of ownership and control over the change taking place. Finally, new metrics, rewards, and milestones must reinforce the accompanying change.

Face Resistance

Finally, leaders must face resistance. This may well be the greatest challenge for all change agents. One of the most effective ways to confront naysayers is to put them in the position where they can experience the problem for themselves. Bill Bratton, the former police commissioner of New York City and Boston, was able to get his constituents to truly understand the crime problem in the New York subway systems after requiring them all to ride the subway for 30 days. They witnessed a multitude of petty crimes and empathized with the nervous subway riders. The facts were indisputable, and officers went to work correcting the problems. Within six months, the transit system was made safer, and there were fewer incidents of crime.

Conger looks to Compaq and Dell as examples of how resistant people are to change. Dell, by using a direct-distribution model, was becoming a force in its industry in the early 1990s. Compaq struggled to keep up after building a powerful retail distribution channel. Compaq did eventually create a direct sales channel but could not find an executive willing to take over the responsibility of leading this charge. Everyone was afraid of rocking the boat; no one wanted to risk upsetting the established balance of power and the existing clients. As a result, Compaq fell far behind Dell.

Bringing about change in any organization is difficult. Resisters are everywhere. Even at the executive level, notes Conger, there can be such extreme competition that many in the top echelon aren't willing to give up their power or comfort level. For any change effort to be successful, it is critical to keep communication channels open so resistance is transparent and leaders can intervene. Change agents are like lighthouses, Conger explains. They signal the direction to follow and serve as both a guide and an alert to danger. The lighthouse of change must operate at full power 24 hours a day, seven days a week.

Reprint B0405D

Short-Term Wins— The Linchpin of a Change Initiative

• • •

You're a year into your company's change initiative, which is designed to boost innovation and focus the company on customer needs. Except for a few cynics, most people seem to be on board. After all the late nights you've spent helping get the initiative up and running, you think it's time to relax a little. But one senior VP refuses to let up. Instead, he launches a six-month project aimed at reducing prototyping costs by a third.

What does he know that you don't? The value of a short-term win.

Even if you've made all the right moves to enlist employees' support for the overall initiative, you still must convince them that the new vision and direction can deliver the goods. Trouble is, a major change initiative can take years, so there's plenty of time to screw up. That's why short-term performance improvements are crucial; they're proof that the change effort can produce results that are superior to the old ways of doing business. The evidence supplied by short-term wins helps overcome the fear and uncertainty that frequently accompany change.

You can start almost anywhere. For example, when the manager of Morgan Bank's microfilm department learned that her unit would have to compete with outside vendors on an equal footing, she identified a service-improvement project that was important to internal customers and that could be accomplished quickly: consistently meeting a 24-hour turnaround requirement for the bank's stock transfer department. This manager had no experience leading a performance-improvement project, so successfully achieving this goal—in five weeks, no less—boosted her confidence immeasurably. Employee support for subsequent changes she initiated increased as well.

But you don't get points for coming close. To be effective, the performance improvement has to be:

- Visible and unambiguous—something that people will readily identify as genuine. Concentrate on high-impact or high-visibility projects that are most likely to succeed. That's exactly what AlliedSignal CEO Larry Bossidy did in rolling out a Six Sigma quality-improvement program. As he explains in *Lessons from the Top,* an upcoming book by Thomas J. Neff and James M. Citrin, "We started it in manufacturing because we thought we had more to gain there."

- Quick—doable in 6–18 months. But don't let the pressure to produce fast, incontrovertible results tempt you to give in to the dark side—to "manufacture" short-term wins by using creative accounting, or by concocting projects that create a buzz but produce nothing substantive. These tricks usually backfire, intensifying resistance to the change effort.

- Clearly related to the change initiative. Sure, a decline in the value of the dollar may be a boon to your company's export sales, but it won't help win people over to the merits of your change effort. By contrast, when General Electric launched its companywide "Work-Out" process to improve its responsiveness to customers, the lighting division began working with a trucking company to schedule regular delivery days for particular customers in advance.

Preparing the Ground

Short-term wins don't simply happen —first you have to do the necessary preparatory work, then plan and monitor with care. In John Kotter's widely accepted model of change, for example, short-term wins constitute the sixth of eight stages.

In the earlier stages, the organization's natural resistance to change is "defrosted": the leader of the initiative establishes a sense of urgency throughout the company. A guiding coalition is assembled to oversee the long and complex effort. A compelling vision, linked to a clear and well-coordinated strategic plan, is articulated and communicated to the far corners of the company. Next comes tearing down organizational barriers: the structures that fragment responsibility and resources, the training and performance-appraisal systems that aren't aligned with the new vision, the management information systems that fail to address market and competitive realities. Individual managers who are resisting the effort need to be confronted—what is expected of them, and when, has to be spelled out. When all this preparatory work is complete, the stage is set for identifying and generating short-term wins.

Managing, Not Leading

Leadership of a change effort involves setting a direction, aligning people with a vision, and motivating them to achieve it. *Management*, by contrast, brings order and consistency—it involves planning, budgeting, and monitoring. A successful change effort, Kotter declares, is 70% to 90% leadership and only 30% to 10% management. But short-term wins are the one area where leadership takes a back seat to management. Use these tips to help you manage the two or three projects you've carved out for your group:

1: Make "Plan, Budget, Monitor" Your Mantra

Break complex tasks down into components, then tackle the simpler components first, making sure you've methodically answered the necessary budgeting, organizing, and staffing questions. Carefully measure and record the improvements as they occur; they'll be harder to document if you wait until the end of the project.

2: Preach Results

Concentrating on systems, structures, processes, activities, and attitudes—what Michael Beer, Russell A. Eisenstat, and Bert Spector call the "programmatic approach to change"—is not the way to go. Instead, focus ruthlessly on solving the concrete business problems embedded in the projects you've identified.

3: Maintain Employees' Disciplined Attention

The future is now—stick to the tasks at hand. Use a sense of urgency as a tool for regulating the workplace equilibrium, writes Ronald A. Heifetz in *Leadership Without Easy Answers*: a certain degree of urgency is galvanizing, but too much is debilitating. In 1992, Sears CEO Arthur

Martinez launched ambitious projects to build a sense of urgency for a massive, multiyear transformation effort aimed at revitalizing the company's retail business. Within two years, Martinez declared, Sears would quadruple operating margins in its retail stores *and* improve customer satisfaction by 15%. This was galvanizing, not debilitating—the company did just that.

Performance improvements like these have more than the obvious short-term motivational benefits. There are also long-term, strategic effects; indeed, Kotter claims that the ability to generate short-term wins 14 and 26 months after the beginning of a change initiative is often a good indicator of whether the initiative will succeed. The empirical data derived from these early projects help senior management refine strategies and timetables, thereby eliminating problems in the next phase of the initiative. Moreover, short-term-win projects can help build organizational capabilities that make for sustainable high performance.

Many change initiatives fail because managers don't believe you can produce major change and achieve excellent short-term results at the same time. That's an outmoded assumption; the one reinforces the other.

For Further Reading

"Why Change Programs Don't Produce Change" by Michael Beer, Russell A. Eisenstat, and Bert Spector (*Harvard Business Review*, May–June 1991).

Leading Change by John P. Kotter (1996, Harvard Business School Press).

Leadership Without Easy Answers by Ronald A. Heifetz (1994, Belknap/Harvard University Press).

Results-Based Leadership: How Leaders Build the Business and Improve the Bottom Line by Dave Ulrich, Jack Zenger, and Norman Smallwood (1999, Harvard Business School Press).

Lessons from the Top: The Search for America's Best Business Leaders by Thomas J. Neff and James M. Citrin (1999, Doubleday).

Reprint U9908A

How to Get Aboard a Major Change Effort

An Interview with John Kotter

• • •

John P. Kotter's 1995 article "Leading Change" quickly jumped to the top of the list of most-requested *Harvard Business Review* reprints—no surprise in an era of continued restructuring. Shortly afterward, the former Harvard Business School Matsushita Professor of Leadership published a book on the subject. In an interview, we asked him to shift perspective slightly and address major change initiatives from the point of view not of those in charge, but rather, of those being led.

Say that you're a manager in an organization, but not in senior management, and suddenly a major change initiative is announced. How should you respond?

It's easy for even a good, well-meaning person to respond the wrong way, maybe because you start thinking pessimistic thoughts, or digging a trench under your desk, which is not in your best interests. We've all got to learn more about fundamental change, to succeed in our own careers, to help the company, to help society. Running away from it is not the answer because we're just going to see more of it coming at us. Maybe the name will be different, maybe in 10 years re-engineering will no longer be the label, but the basic phenomenon will only continue and increase because of the powerful macroeconomic forces at work.

The other mistake, almost the opposite of the first, is the naive "Oh, wonderful, now we're finally going to change this place." It's naive in the sense that you think it's not going to be hard work, or take a long time, or require a lot of skill from a lot of people. So you charge into it, try to do too much too fast, and fall on your face. Or if you're really naive, you get set up by the political forces who don't want to change anything anyway; they would love to have it all blow up and are happy to have a fall guy.

What should your stance be? The more you get it into your head that this is not an aberration, that these kinds of large changes inside organizations are not just an ego trip on the part of a senior person, but are systematically a part of broader forces, the more your attitude will be "I've got to get better at this stuff." You will want to learn how to be a more skilled, perceptive, able change agent yourself. Like any other set of complex skills, this isn't something you're going to learn in a two-day workshop. You'll learn mostly on the job, by trial and error. You should stop and ask yourself, "How do I learn best?" Is it from good role models? Then search around and see if you can find within the company a major change that worked and try to find out how the people roughly in your position handled it. What mistakes did they make? What did they do right?

So people who are not on the top team leading the effort have to become change agents themselves?

With two or three of these major change efforts under way at the same time in some organizations, even middle-level managers are being drawn into this, and not just as passive followers of some great leader. They're being asked to take their thing, even if that thing is just five employees, and restructure it, to develop and implement a totally new strategy for their little operation. Leading change, which once was only the domain of the Jack Welchs, has increasingly become central to middle managers and their career success.

When you hear the first announcement of a change effort, what should you be listening for?

If there's a real vision higher up, the clearer you can get that in your head, the better off you'll be. Not the tactics—where people get screwed up is they don't get the vision, and therefore they think they're trying to help, but they're actually going at a 30 degree angle to the thrust.

How do you get greater clarity on the vision?

You talk around. You try to figure out not one person but what group of people you're comfortable with who might have a slant on this or some information that you don't have. Some people have a good enough relationship with their boss that they can sit down and say, "I want to help with this 100%, and the clearer that I have it in my mind what the overall goal is, the more I'm going to be able to help. Let me tell you what I've heard so far, and you correct me." A lot of people can't do that; they don't have that kind of relationship with the boss. Then they have to work on other angles, say, by going to peers they think may have a good take on what's going on.

How many change efforts actually work?

It's a continuum, it's not on-off. If you were to grade them using the old fashioned A, B, C, D, and F, I'd be surprised if an impartial jury would give 10% of these efforts an A. But I'm not saying that 90% deserve a D–

either. What is tragic is that there are so many C+'s. It's one thing to get a C+ on a paper; it's another when millions of dollars or thousands of jobs are at stake . . . C+, when the stakes are like that, is just not good enough.

Isn't it important to figure out whether the effort in your organization is going to be A– or C+?

Of course. My advice on that may be a bit radical: Who wants to hang around a C+ organization? Everybody should try to find a place where they can contribute to a winning effort because you learn more, find more rewards, and feel better about yourself. So if you honestly think the effort is going to fail on 16 different dimensions, you should seriously think about getting out of there. If it's a big company, think about moving to another part of the organization.

People say, "But what about my health care?" That's myopic. The deal these days is learning, learning, learning. We've all got to be learning more, keeping on that ramp that most of us were on as kids. If you're in an organization that's consistently doing C+, you've got no good role models to learn from.

What's your responsibility to your subordinates after a change initiative has been announced?

You've got to get it clear in your head before you start talking to the troops. Once it's clear in your mind what this effort is all about, and what role your unit is going

> ## "Recognize that the forces that maintain the status quo are powerful and everywhere."

to play in it, and therefore what you need from these subordinates, and you get to the point where you start believing it—and if you don't, you ought to seriously think about finding a home you can believe in—you're in a much better position to sit down with your people and talk to them meaningfully, field their questions, deal with their anxieties, and help them get into it in a positive way.

What happens when you hear the announcement—the CEO says, "We're going to be pioneers in interstellar commerce"— and you know it just ain't going to work?

Then the question becomes "How can we get some valid information to decision makers, and in a way that doesn't get us all killed in the process?" The people who are good at this don't go marching in to the boss, face red, and pound on tables. They look for ways that can, without them necessarily being in the center of it, get valid information aggregated in a credible way and shipped on to the desks of the important people. This is one of the ways consultants earn a living. You've got consultants working on a project and you quietly make sure that they look at this stuff, and you don't send the report to the bosses, but they do. At the extreme, if you can't figure out a way to do that, before you start building the interstellar cruiser, you might think about other employment.

You mentioned the possibility of being set up by the forces who oppose the change. How do you watch out for that?

The key thing there is to not get paranoid. On the other hand, the better you can think through who is not, at least at first, going to like this change, and why, and the more you watch those people, the lower the probability that you're going to get the arrow in the back because you're going to be facing them. You must recognize that the forces in organizations that maintain the status quo are powerful and everywhere. Don't demonize them, though, or think of them as the enemy, because they sincerely think the effort is stupid. You just have to be careful that somebody from one of those groups doesn't see you as a ringleader.

Is there any way to diagnose whether, as part of the change effort, you are changing enough yourself?

The best way is to find people you trust and ask them. Say, "This is the issue. I think I'm on board and I'm helping, but I know I could be blind and that I'm dragging my feet. Do you see any signs of that?"

What can you do if you worry that the change initiative is too top-down, that the people who will have to carry it out haven't really been consulted?

Instead of saying, "This is what we're going to do," say, "This is what they're thinking of right now; what do you see?" The best department heads initiate the meeting to get the ideas from the grass roots; they don't wait for the big bosses to tell them to do it. They figure out what they can act on themselves without waiting for permission from above. You don't have to be a mindless link in a top-down chain of information; you can stop the flow of information and inject your mind, and other minds, into it.

> "Increasingly, followers have to be leaders, too."

What about the real corporate hard cases? How do you deal with subordinates who have seen the TQM effort that was C+, then re-engineering, then a succession of other less-than-successful initiatives?

You start by asking yourself, "Is this going to be another C+?" If the answer is "No," you need to marshal in your own mind the evidence that the people at the top are going about it differently this time, and sit down and talk it out with your people. You don't overcome cynicism with cynical manipulation; you disarm it by being disarmingly candid—"Let's face it, guys, just within these four walls, that last quality project was a bomb. Let's try to think why. And let me try to explain why I believe this new one may be better." If you're willing to be candid, and to take the blows from the crowd, you may find that this kind of discussion at least begins to move people toward the neutral zone. You're not going to have everybody carrying you off on their shoulders, but at least you've lessened the resistance, and that's a real service.

Say that you realize that the inevitable conclusion of the change effort will be to eliminate your division and your job. Then what do you do?

Almost any answer to that will sound a bit cavalier. What's the alternative? Is the answer to try to hang in there and become a better dinosaur, or to block something that's really in the company's best interest to save your job. No. 1: That's tough to do. No. 2: You're not going to feel good about it. The only alternative is to figure out some way to move forward—don't just watch it happen; instead, remind yourself about what careers are about today. Careers are no longer about "I go to work for some place forever." They're becoming much more dynamic. Part of why we fear "Oh my gosh, they're going to eliminate this group" is that we grew up in a world where the hiring folks were suspicious of any breaks in your career progress. That's not the future. If anything, we're seeing increasing suspicion if a résumé looks too linear, stable, and slick because that's not the world we're living in. The proper stance is "How do I turn this into a terrific learning experience so that when I go on to the next stage, I'll have more skills plus this track record?" You want to be able to say, "I helped with this effort and as a matter of fact its end result was eliminating my own job—but by God, I did the right thing, and it helped the company." That's a terrific pitch in getting your next job.

We're told that managers need to be loyal to their individual disciplines, skills, and projects, and not expect 30 years with the company. Change efforts benefit the organization, not necessarily the individual. Isn't there a tension between those two imperatives?

There is a tension, but the solution is not an either-or one. The solution has got to be "all of the above." People need to worry about themselves and their own skill sets, but they also need to worry about customers, the price of the stock, the suppliers. It's not good enough any more to say, "I'll be a good corporate man," or to say, "I'll just look out for myself." You've got to do both, plus.

What if you conclude that you'll be all right after the change, but your people may be eliminated. What's your responsibility to them?

In this current world of change, you do have a responsibility to these people but it isn't to protect their status quo. Your responsibility is to help them grow and position themselves for a better future. There may be cases where you have to talk them out of their own parochialness. You may want to say to them, "This is an opportunity for all of us and if we do a good job, we'll all be employable. And I'll help. I'll testify that you did the right thing and you learned a lot, and they should be lucky to have you working with them."

I had a former student come see me recently. He was moving into a tough job, a turnaround, and he had a list of concerns. After listening to him for 20 minutes I said, "The biggest single piece of advice I could give you is to keep in mind the main point, which is that you've got a company here that could go down the tubes—lost jobs, lost portfolio value, hurt customers, hurt suppliers.

You've signed on to not let that happen. Each and every day you should be going into your office saying, 'What have I done today to help make better and better products and services that serve real customer needs at lower and lower costs and prices so we can help save this sucker?'"

Is there anything different about followership these days from, say, 10 years ago?

Increasingly, followers have to be leaders, too. This whole notion of "I'm just a middle manager, I'm not a leader in this company" is bad—bad for the people, bad for the company. To be sure, you're not the CEO, but in a non-static world, you not only have to be good at something professionally—marketing, for instance—and at managing, to make sure things function as they should. You're also going to be asked to provide leadership to make your organization more dynamic, more global, and to take on new technologies. Stop thinking about leadership as just something that Churchill did.

For Further Reading

Leading Change by John P. Kotter (1996, Harvard Business School Press).

Reprint U9609B

Change through Appreciative Inquiry

• • •

Tom Krattenmaker

Alarmed by a weakening market position and declining staff morale, Really Rapid Transit, Inc. needed to change. Senior management called in organizational experts to diagnose the problems and prescribe solutions. The consultants crafted a plan that would change everything from employee uniforms to customer interaction to the way data got entered. But when it came time for the rollout, Really Rapid's employees balked.

Stinging from the implied and direct criticism in the consultants' report, they weren't the least bit interested in a set of changes they found threatening. Wasn't this, they asked, just the latest ham-handed nonsense imposed by their out-of-touch bosses?

Meanwhile, at Enlightened Lighting, Inc., management and staff approached the change process a different way. Employees came together to talk not about problems and solutions, but their greatest successes. What was it like, they were asked, when this organization was at its best? Staff members told stories and reviewed them together to glean common themes. The company then conceived a vision of what it might achieve in the brightest possible future and, working backwards from that, devised the steps and resources that would enable them to realize the vision. When the plan was completed, the employees eagerly embarked on the new course as full partners with management.

Enlightened Lighting was using appreciative inquiry, an approach to organizational change that emphasizes and builds on a company's strengths and potential. Based on social constructionism—the theory that people and organizations create their realities through their interpretations of and conversations about the world—AI was first developed in the 1980s by David Cooperrider of Case Western Reserve University and is being used by a growing number of corporations and non-profit organizations around the world.

"The more you focus on *problems*, the more you slow yourself down," says Jane Magruder Watkins, a leading AI practitioner and coauthor (with Bernard J. Mohr) of the book *Appreciative Inquiry: Change at the Speed of Imagination*. "The more you seek out what works and create images of where you want to go, the better able you'll be to keep up with the ever-increasing rate of change. The old model is about fixing up the status quo. That's not good enough anymore. By the time you solve one set of problems, 900 more things are wrong."

Kenneth Gergen, a Swarthmore College psychology professor credited with developing social constructionism, says that the way people talk about their organizations shapes their behavior within them. "It's not clear how much is to be gained from a problem orientation," says Gergen. "You can find problems everywhere when you start looking. If you take it too far, you create a sense that it's all insurmountable. But if we could construct a world in which something is *possible*, we can talk about that in such a way that we might be able to achieve it together. Suddenly, you create a tremendous positive energy."

Consider one example of appreciative inquiry in action. The corporate finance division at Bank of Scotland used AI to transform its internal communications. The bank's leaders knew they needed to create two-way information flow between managers and front-line employees, both to keep them up to speed and to draw from their experience and knowledge. Not interested in identifying problems—project designers feared that would devolve into deflating "whine sessions"—the bank instead held 10 workshops to explore what the company did best and why.

As reported by employee communication manager Ruth Findlay in the February 2001 issue of the *AI Newsletter*, each of the workshops was composed of a mix of people from most departments and all salary grades. Working in pairs, participants interviewed one another about particular instances in the previous six months when they felt energized by the contribution they were making to the bank. They then explored the ingredients of the high moments. The stories were collected and analyzed for common standards of communication and positive actions that could be taken to bring about change.

Out of the stories came a report called "100 Voices," which mapped out how the division would achieve a quality of internal communications that matched the excellence it had already achieved in corporate finance.

"The information that's needed in an organization is alive at every level," says Watkins. "It's no longer the case that people at the top know what's best. Most good leaders realize that they really need to access all the intelligence of their organization. AI gives you the ability to do that. It's extremely democratic."

Watkins identifies five core principles that have evolved

into what she calls the "DNA of appreciative inquiry."
They are:

THE CONSTRUCTIONIST PRINCIPLE: an organization's
destiny is bound up in people's understanding of it.
The first task in changing an organization is to
discover what its people think about it.

THE PRINCIPLE OF SIMULTANEITY: the process of
inquiry itself influences the direction of change.

THE ANTICIPATORY PRINCIPLE: the most powerful
vehicle for improving an organization is the collective
imagination about its future, about what it is
becoming.

THE POETIC PRINCIPLE: an organization's "story" is
constantly being rewritten by everyone within the
organization and everyone who interacts with it. The
organization, like a poem, is constantly being
interpreted and reinterpreted.

THE POSITIVE PRINCIPLE: an inquiry based on the
positive—achievement, joy, hope, and inspiration—
works better than an analysis of what is wrong and
how it can be cured.

Anne Radford, a London-based AI practitioner and
editor of the *AI Newsletter*, emphasizes that appreciative inquiry depends very much on the participation of

everyone in an organization: "Appreciative inquiry isn't something that is done to employees," she says. "They are not on the receiving end of a process. They *are* the process."

Watkins and Mohr suggest the following five steps in an appreciative inquiry process.

1: Make the Focus of Inquiry Positive

When an organization embarks on a course of inquiry and change, it can either collect and analyze data, identify obstacles, and make diagnoses—the traditional approach—or it can seek out what is good and right about the organization. The difference is in the questions that are asked. A company interested in improving client relations could ask: "What can we do to minimize client anger and complaints?" In an AI process, the question instead would be: "When have customers been most pleased with our service, and what can we learn and apply from those moments of success?"

2: Elicit Positive Stories

The second step uses interviews to evoke stories that illuminate an organization's distinctive strengths. When the organization is functioning at its best, what characteristics are present? Positive stories, unlike data or lists, stir imaginations and generate excitement about the company and what it is capable of accomplishing in the future. A change process based on telling and hearing such stories is energizing, Radford says, "because it builds on what is already working."

3: Locate Themes That Appear in the Stories

The goal is not to choose the best stories, nor those that represent the norm. Rather, the purpose is to find what elements are common to the moments of greatest success and fulfillment, and are also most promising and inspiring as components of a desired future. "The themes become the basis for collectively imagining what the organization would be like if the exceptional moments we have uncovered in the interviews become the norm in the organization," Watkins says.

4: Create Shared Images for the Future

Riding on the momentum of Step Three, this stage in the process asks organization members to create a future in which the high points identified in the stories are the everyday reality. In addition to "articulating the dream," as Watkins phrases it, the team designs the structure—the policies, business processes, resources,

etc.—for achieving the desired future. Pieces of the structure could include such elements as the acquisition and
use of a powerful new technology or the commitment to
designing a performance appraisal system that rewards
rather than punishes.

5: Find Innovative Ways
to Create That Future

Finally, organization members identify and carry out
measures to put flesh on the skeleton created in Step
Four; they find creative ways to bring the preferred
future to life. This could mean a new way of communicating with customers or provocative new management
training programs. For example, a health care organization emerged from this phase of its AI process with a
new program for honoring exemplary customer service,
a system for soliciting and implementing employees'
suggestions, and a more streamlined decision-making
mechanism.

Susan Wood, who left her position with a major consulting firm to start a practice dedicated to appreciative
inquiry, believes AI can be especially effective for employee retention. Wood, who is based in the Philadelphia
area, is using the approach in her work with a hospital
concerned about rapid turnover in its nursing ranks.
Rather than trying to figure out why nurses are leaving,
she and her partners have set out to discover why those

who remain are staying. What they've found is a fierce loyalty to the profession of nursing. Among the policies that have emerged are an employee recognition program, a mentoring program, and a new approach to orientation that emphasizes the noble aspects of nursing.

"These nurses were very beaten-down and overworked," Wood says. "But as soon as we started them in a conversation about what they were good at, the tone changed. We've been able to work with them without resistance or complaining. They've gotten on board. And they're coming up with things that are going to work."

Watkins predicts that appreciative inquiry will continue to grow in popularity as the workplace changes. "Once you get this process going, people have this 'A-ha' experience," she says. "They've been wanting a different kind of workplace, one that provides fulfillment and inspiration as well as a paycheck. Appreciative inquiry gives them that, and it makes them the primary means by which it's created."

For Further Reading

Appreciative Inquiry: Change at the Speed of Imagination by Jane Magruder Watkins and Bernard J. Mohr (2001, Jossey-Bass).

Reprint C0110B

Organization Capital I

Supporting the Change Agenda That Supports Strategy Execution

• • •

Robert S. Kaplan and David P. Norton

Managing strategy is about managing change. A strategy describes how an organization intends to create value for its stakeholders. And the strategy map defines and clarifies the logic of this value creation process: how a customer value proposition will lead to shareholder rewards, how a set of processes will support this value proposition, and how a set of intangible assets (people and technology) will enable these processes. But unless the organization is able to execute the changes described by this logic, the strategy is worthless. We refer to this ability of the organization to mobilize and sustain the process of change required to execute the strategy as *organization capital*. Organization capital, along with human capital and information capital, constitutes the intangible assets of an enterprise.

Organization capital enables integration, so that not only are individual intangible assets (human and information capital) and tangible assets (physical and financial) aligned to the strategy, but all are integrated, working together to achieve the organization's strategic objectives. An enterprise with high organization capital has a shared understanding of vision, mission, values, and strategy; is led with strength; has created a performance culture around the strategy; and shares knowledge up, down, and across so that everyone works together and in the same direction. Conversely, an enterprise with low organization capital has failed to communicate its priorities and establish the new culture. The ability to create positive organization capital is one of the best predictors of successful strategy execution.

Most organizations in our research database of strategy maps and Balanced Scorecards identify three to five organization capital objectives in their learning and growth perspective; typical objectives include "build leaders," "align the workforce," "share knowledge," and "focus on the customer." But setting these objectives is usually an ad hoc and intuitive effort. Executives do not have a general framework in which to focus their thinking on organizational culture and climate, and, in particular, align it to the strategy. Yet despite the absence of such a framework and the considerable diversity of approaches, we have identified important common elements used by most executives. We have synthesized these elements into a new, albeit still exploratory, framework for describing and measuring organization capital.

Organization capital is typically built upon four components:

CULTURE: All employees are aware of and internalize the mission, vision, and core values needed to execute the strategy.

LEADERSHIP: Qualified leaders are available at all levels to mobilize the organization toward its strategy.

ALIGNMENT: Individual, team, and departmental goals and incentives are linked to the attainment of strategic objectives.

TEAMWORK: Knowledge (with strategic potential) is shared throughout organization.

The strategy map describes how a new strategy requires change, such as new products, new processes, or new customers. These changes, in turn, define new behaviors and values that are required of the workforce. The first step in developing an organization capital strategy is to define the *organization change agenda* implied by the broader strategy. This change agenda identifies the shifts in organization climate necessary to effect the strategy. The objectives fall into two categories of behavioral changes: those required to create value for customers and shareholders, and those required to execute the strategy. Three different kinds of behavior changes are consistently highlighted for *creating* value:

- Focus on the customer

- Be creative and innovative

- Deliver results

Four additional behavior changes are associated with executing strategy:

- Understand the mission, vision, and values

- Create accountability

- Communicate openly

- Work as a team

No one organization has incorporated all seven of these into its change agenda. Typically, an organization will identify two to four of these objectives for its scorecard. For example, companies in deregulated industries like utilities or telecommunications place a heavy emphasis on becoming customer-focused and innovative because these are totally new behaviors for them. Previously, their culture involved little more than operating efficiently, avoiding risks, and negotiating effectively with regulators so that revenues from their monopoly position would cover their costs. Pharmaceutical companies, long driven by functional and disciplinary capabilities that supported their innovation strategy, now strive to become more customer-focused and to foster teamwork to share knowledge across the organization. Thus, the change agenda identifies the three or four most important behavioral changes required for the new strategy to be implemented.

Using the organization change agenda as the linkage between strategy and organization capital, we can examine its four components—culture, leadership, alignment, and teamwork—in more detail. Here, we focus on culture.

Culture

Culture reflects the predominant attitudes and behaviors that characterize how a group or organization functions. "Shaping the culture" is the most often cited priority in the Learning and Growth section of our Balanced Scorecard database. Executives generally believe that: (1) strategy requires basic changes in the way organizations conduct business; (2) strategy must be executed through individuals at all levels of the organization; and, hence, (3) new attitudes and behaviors—culture—will be required throughout the workforce as a prerequisite for these changes.

Culture can be a barrier or an enabler. Studies have shown that a large percentage of mergers and acquisitions fail to deliver synergies,[1] and a prime reason for this is cultural incompatibility. Yet a company like Cisco is renowned for its ability to integrate newly acquired companies into its culture. IBM Services and Electronic Data Systems (EDS) have built large, successful outsourcing businesses while assimilating the staff of outsourced units into their culture. Does culture dictate strategy, or does strategy dictate culture? We believe it's the latter. In the case of companies such as Cisco, IBM, and EDS, the ability to assimilate new organizations into the company culture is clearly an asset for their growth strategies. Most strategies, however, are not about assimilating newly acquired organizations into an existing culture. They require dramatic changes in a company's existing culture. The leadership team must introduce new attitudes and behaviors in all employees for the new strategy to be successful.

Consider the experience of Information Management Services (IMS), the internal IT department of a major telecommunications company in the early 1990s. With the telecom industry undergoing deregulation, the parent company had converted IMS from a cost center to a

> The beauty . . . of the Balanced Scorecard is that the act of measurement forces somewhat vague and ambiguous concepts such as culture and climate to be defined more precisely.

profit center. Virtually overnight, IMS had to transform itself from the captive supplier of a monopoly customer in a regulated industry—where cost increases could be recovered through higher rates—to a freestanding unit that would be customer-focused and market-competitive, competing for external as well as internal customers. Long-standing culture, values, and management approaches had in an instant become obsolete. Moreover, this radical cultural transformation had to occur in the midst of a technological disruption, one that had shifted the platform for information technology from centralized, mainframe-based services to distributed, mobile client-server computing. And customers had changed, too; now they were looking to their IT supplier for solutions, not merely new technology.

In the past, IMS could recover its costs through overhead allocations imposed by the corporate parent on its operating divisions. Now IMS had to earn profits and acquire business based on competitive fees, responsiveness, and value-added services for customers. A new culture of results delivery had to be established. The implications for cultural change were obvious and dramatic. The new IMS could no longer view its customers as "captives." It had to compete against companies such as EDS, Accenture, and IBM by convincing customers, internal and external, that it was the preferred knowledgeable partner. IMS had to shift from measuring success by delivering system enhancements on budget and on schedule to becoming an action-oriented, entrepreneurial, and knowledgeable partner with its customers, helping them get bottom-line benefits from IT solutions. These new attitudes and behaviors were fundamental to the success of the strategy. IMS would have to introduce many changes to make this strategy happen. New technologies, new processes, and new skills were required. But unless these changes were accompanied by the cultural shifts entailed in transforming from captive supplier to profit-seeking entrepreneur, the strategy was doomed to fail.

Matching Change Objectives to the Strategy

We have seen many organizations embark on a cultural shift as dramatic as that faced by IMS. Among the most common cultural change objectives is *customer focus*. It is also the most frequently identified change at service companies—telecommunications, financial, healthcare, transportation, energy, and utilities organizations—that began competing in deregulated environments. Employees had to learn that customers, not regulators, create value. Organization A, a regional health plan, attempted to create a customer-centric culture for executives by emphasizing "time spent by leadership with customers." Front-line employees were already close to customers, but executives also needed to spend time with customers if they were to become more effective leaders. Organization B, a regional bank,wanted its employees to become solutions-oriented, not transaction-oriented, so that they could build closer consulting relations with targeted customers.

While *customer focus* would seem most appropriate for companies shifting to a total customer solutions strategy, we have also seen objectives that relate to other strategies. For example, companies competing on consistency and reliability will likely want to establish a culture of *quality* and *continuous improvement*. A culture of *continuous cost reduction* would be relevant for companies competing on low total cost, especially with nondifferentiated products. And companies striving to maintain product leadership want to establish a culture of *creativity* and *product innovation*. Even with these alternative cultures, though, employees must remain focused on customers and how the value propositions they create and deliver add value to targeted customers.

Innovation/risk-taking objectives send a message to the workforce that it's OK to challenge the status quo. Organizations C and D, both deregulated utilities, used words like "entrepreneur," "innovation," and "creativity" to stress the behaviors required in their new world.

Organizations introducing shareholder value programs want a culture focused on *results.* Organization E, a chemicals company, wanted to shift its employees from an engineering culture to one that could apply technology to deliver financial results. Organization F, another newly deregulated utility, used the phrase "produce results" to signal that the measure of success had changed.

Understanding mission and strategy is an important objective for organizations of functional specialists who must strike a balance between maintaining excellence within their silos while simultaneously integrating with other parts of the enterprise. Organization G, a health plan, wanted to improve performance by more closely integrating its medical staff with its administrative staff. Organization H, a professional services firm, had its technology group introduce innovative Web-based consulting services that appeared, on the surface, to threaten the company's consultants, who had grown accustomed to delivering results only through face-to-face interactions with clients.

Accountability plays an important role in organizations that historically have been internally focused or highly regulated and then must become customer- and market-focused. Organization I is a manufacturing company with international customers and a global network of manufacturing plants and suppliers. Formerly, I had defined executive responsibilities by function and used cost-based transfer prices to measure success for manufacturing units along the supply chain. No one was accountable for end-to-end profitability and performance. I's new strategy simplified the organization, provided more sourcing and buying discretion, and measured the performance of each unit with market-based prices for inputs and outputs.

Open communications is an important objective for strategies that require a high degree of integration. Organization J, a pharmaceutical company, was attempting to accelerate the flow of knowledge and marketplace experience from its commercial division to its product development group.

Teamwork is important on the change agenda when a strategy redefines the role of different units. Organization K, a multidivisional manufacturing company with many stand-alone brands, wanted to create synergy among these brands through more marketplace integration. The term "dual citizenship" communicates the simultaneous role for a distinct brand to also be part of a corporate image. Organization L used the mantra "one team, one dream" to show how different branch offices, with somewhat different local objectives, still contributed to the success of the global corporate strategy.

Measuring Culture

Measurement of cultural values relies heavily on employee surveys. The beauty—but also the complexity—of the Balanced Scorecard is that the act of measurement forces somewhat vague and ambiguous concepts such as culture and climate to be defined more precisely.

Organizational behavior expert Charles O'Reilly and his colleagues have developed a measurement instrument, the Organizational Culture Profile (OCP)[2] that contains a set of statements that describe possible values of an organization. Employees are asked to rank 54 value statements according to their perceived importance and relevance in the organization. From these rankings an organization's culture can be mapped, with an acceptable degree of reliability and validity, into eight independent factors:

- Innovation and risk taking

- Attention to detail

- Results-focused

- Aggressiveness and competitiveness

- Supportiveness [of the individual employee]

- Growth and rewards

- Collaboration and teamwork

- Decisiveness

The OCP statements are based on norms, people's expectations about specific attitudes and behaviors. They ask people to respond to questions such as, "What does it really take to get ahead?" and "What are the unwritten rules around here?" A consensus within a unit or organization on the responses represents the culture of the unit. The organization can assess whether the culture is consistent with its strategy. A lack of consensus reflects a lack of a common culture.

Different cultures may be required in different parts of the organization. The culture within the R&D group should be different from that of the manufacturing group; an emergent business unit should have a different culture from that of a mature business unit. Variations from norms are desirable, depending on function and business strategy. But executives likely will want organization-wide agreement around such values as integrity, respect, and treatment of employees. These are the markers of the corporatewide culture.

The existence of an instrument like the OCP indicates that culture has now become a measurable construct. But instruments like the OCP have been influenced by a psychology literature that stresses constructs such as motivation and climate. Since the strategy literature has not perceived culture as being essential for effective strategy implementation, none of the existing instruments that measure culture capture individuals' beliefs and understanding of the strategy. To align the culture dimension more closely to an organization's strategy, rather than just its way of conducting its day-to-day business, the value statements in an OCP-type instrument should be modified to allow employees to evaluate a company on the dimensions identified here, including the value proposition underlying the strategy. We have suggested possibilities such as whether the culture is primarily about continuous improvement and quality programs, or creativity and innovation, or a deep understanding of individual customers' preferences and needs. Developing improved instruments for measuring culture along dimensions relevant to the strategy is clearly an opportunity for further work.[3] Alternatively, organizations will have to develop and rely on ad hoc questionnaires of their own to measure this important dimension.

The Foremost Change Agent

Culture is the foremost factor influencing an organization's ability to change. Thus, culture must be tailored to support the strategy. Different strategies call for different values: new ways of working with customers, peers, the chain of command, suppliers, regulators, and so on. To successfully execute strategy, an organization must be clear about the new values it requires—and must ensure that they are adopted.

Notes

1. S. Chaudhuri and B. Tabrizi, "Capturing the Real Value in High-Tech Acquisitions," *Harvard Business Review* (September–October 1999).

2. C. O'Reilly, J. Chatman, and D. Caldwell, "People and Organizational Culture: A Profile Comparison Approach to Assessing Person-Organization Fit," *Academy of Management Journal* (September 1991).

3. For example, see the approaches available at ThinkShed (www.thinkshed.com), which draws upon the scholarly work of O'Reilly, Chatman, and Caldwell.

Reprint B0401A

Organization Capital II

Leadership, Alignment, and Teamwork

• • •

Robert S. Kaplan and David P. Norton

We've said it often: managing strategy is synonymous with managing change. And it's through intangible assets—organization capital—that an organization mobilizes and sustains the change necessary to execute strategy.

Leadership

When a company changes its strategy, its people must do things differently as well. And it is the job of leaders at all levels of the organization to help employees identify and understand the changes needed to execute the new strategy and to motivate and guide them toward new ways of working.

A change agenda defines the specific shifts in organization climate required by the new strategy. Through our Balanced Scorecard (BSC) research database we've identified seven generic behaviors that executives have typically cultivated as part of their BSC implementations. (See *Figure 1*, left column.) Since each organization and its strategy are different, the organization change agenda must obviously be tailored to each situation. Another important function of the change agenda is that it helps clarify the leader's job.

To ensure that it gets the kind of leaders needed to execute the strategy, the organization should create a Leadership Competency Model. This model identifies the specific traits that leaders must exhibit to support the strategy and is derived directly from the organization change agenda.

Figure 1 illustrates the Leadership Competency Profile for Finco, a disguised financial services company. Finco provides a complex array of financial instruments to corporate investors as part of its strategy of providing a "total customer solution." In reviewing the strategy, we identified eight behavioral changes that Finco leaders were responsible for mobilizing. As shown in *Figure 1*, the changes began with an emphasis on delivering "high-quality solutions that meet clients' business needs," to focus on delivering value to the client. Outstanding leaders were expected to practice this behavior themselves and inculcate it in others. The strategy also called for building long-term relationships. Helping clients solve problems required a more innovative environment

FIGURE 1

The Leadership Competency Model at Finco

Behaviors that create value	Organization change agenda (generic model)	Finco's Leadership Competency Profile
		• **Focus on client value** Outstanding leaders deliver high-quality solutions that meet clients' business needs
	• Focus on the customer	• **Cultivate key relationships** Outstanding leaders build and maintain relationships that promote Finco's market presence
	• Be creative and innovative	• **Drive innovation** Outstanding leaders promote innovation; they are open to change
	• Deliver results	• **Deliver results** Outstanding leaders deliver superior results to all stakeholders
Behaviors that help execute strategy	• Understand the mission, vision, and values	• **Shaping strategy** Outstanding leaders understand how vision is implemented through function-related strategies that achieve sustainable competitive advantage
	• Create alignment and creativity	• **Building commitment** Outstanding leaders communicate openly, gaining support of others, to support Finco's vision and core values
	• Communicate openly	• **Fostering teamwork** Outstanding leaders create teamwork across individuals, organizations, and cultures
	• Work as a team	• **Fostering organization learning** Outstanding leaders ensure continuity of the business through knowledge transfer and increasing intellectual capital

The eight competencies identified in Finco's Leadership Competency Profile helped the company achieve its "total customer solution" strategy.

75

than Finco had previously established, as well as a focus on results. Besides these five value-creating behaviors, leaders were also expected to build competencies that would improve the organization's ability to execute strategy: translating the vision ("shaping strategy") into discrete functional plans to which employees could align themselves; spurring open communications to build commitment; fostering teamwork and promoting knowledge transfer ("fostering organization learning") rounded out the list of desired leadership competencies.

Organizations will typically use employee surveys to see how an executive measures up against the ideal traits listed in the Leadership Competency Profile. A staffer might solicit information from subordinates, peers, and superiors about a leader's mastery of the critical skills; an external unit might also solicit such input. This feedback is used mainly for coaching and developing the leader, but an organizational unit can also aggregate the detailed (and confidential) data from the individual reviews to create a status report on leadership competencies needed throughout the organization.

Alignment

Organizational change expert Peter Senge, in *The Fifth Discipline: The Art and Practice of the Learning Organization*, stresses that broad-based organizational change requires alignment in which all members of a team have a com-

monality of purpose, a shared vision, and an understanding of how their personal roles support the overall
strategy. "Alignment is the necessary condition before
empowering [the individual]. . . . [Once aligned] the individual will empower the whole team."[1] An aligned organization encourages employee empowerment, innovation, and risk taking because individual actions are
directed at achieving high-level objectives. Encouraging
and empowering individual initiative in an unaligned
organization leads to chaos, as the innovative risk takers
pull the organization in contradictory directions. The
effect is similar to that of the self-declared job description of a new business school dean: "taking 60 puppy
dogs for a walk without a leash."

Achieving alignment is a two-step process. First, leaders must communicate the organization's high-level
strategic objectives in ways that every employee can understand. Second, leaders must ensure that individuals and
teams have local objectives (with associated rewards)
that, if achieved, contribute to achieving the targets of
the high-level objectives. Leaders create strategic awareness through a multifaceted communications program
involving a wide range of channels—brochures, newsletters, town hall meetings, orientation and training
programs, executive talks, intranets, and bulletin boards.
Organizations typically use employee surveys to determine whether employees are aware of and understand
the high-level strategic objectives. *Figure 2* shows how several organizations measure alignment. Organization A,

FIGURE 2

Measuring Alignment and Teamwork: Typical Measures

Organization capital	Strategic Objective
	• Ensure all employees understand the strategy
	• Reinforce strategic direction and strengthen sense of urgency and purpose
Alignment	• Align efforts through measurement and reward
	• Align personal goals
	• Create a motivated and prepared workforce
	• Empower employees
	• Develop a learning organization
	• Continually develop and transfer knowledge
Teamwork (knowledge sharing)	• Ensure communication of best-practice ideas
	• Improve cross-company communication
	• Create and utilize a common global system and process for sharing knowledge
	• Ensure availability of accurate, consistent information across the organization
	• Integrate employees

Here's how a variety of actual organizations define and measure alignment and teamwork (knowledge sharing).

a healthcare provider, uses a portion of its annual employee survey to quantify the percentage of employees who can identify the organization's strategic priorities. Other organizations sample employee awareness more

Strategic Measure	Organization
• Percentage of employees who can identify the organization's strategic priorities (survey)	Healthcare (A)
• Percentage of employees with objectives tied to BSC	Mutual funds (B)
• Percentage of employees with goals mapped to strategy (BSC)	Healthcare (C)
• Percentage of staff with goals linked to BSC	National bank (D)
• Percentage of staff with personal BSC	Process manufacturing (E)
• Percentage of staff with training and development linked to BSC	City government (F)
• Number of best practices identified • Output per employee	Chemicals (G)
• Hours of training per person	Mutual insurance (H)
• Percentage of employees participating in the "work-out" process	Financial services (I)
• Percentage of staff using knowledge-sharing channels	Pharmaceuticals (J)
• Currency of projects in knowledge bank (KB) • Number of hits to KB	Software (K)
• Percentage of targeted measures, data, and statistics accessible across the organization	Financial services (L)
• Number of cross-division movements	Manufacturing (M)

frequently, measuring the effectiveness of their employee education program in the same way they would measure an advertising campaign aimed at potential customers.

Organizations also achieve strategic alignment by linking employees' individual objectives and the reward/recognition system to business unit and corporate objectives. Organization B, a mutual funds company, Organization C, another healthcare company, and Organization D, a national bank, all modified their personal goal-setting processes when they introduced the BSC. They educated employees about the organization's strategy and Balanced Scorecard, then asked them to link their personal objectives to the enterprise scorecard. The companies monitored the progress of this program by measuring the percentage of employees with objectives linked to the BSC. Organization E, a process manufacturing company, pushed the alignment idea further, requiring every employee to build his own Balanced Scorecard. Finally, Organization F, a city government, had already linked employee goals to the Balanced Scorecard. Currently in year three of its program, the organization now uses the Balanced Scorecard to align its training and development program to the strategy. It measures the percentage of staff with training and development linked to the BSC.

A sports team would never enter the field of play until every player understood the game plan; otherwise, there would be chaos. Organizations must make the same effort to ensure that every employee understands the strategy. The extent to which they succeed in achieving this alignment determines the value of their organization capital.

Teamwork (Knowledge Sharing)

There is no greater waste than a good idea used only once. And there is no asset with greater potential for an organization than the collective knowledge of its employees. Many companies today use formal knowledge management systems to generate, organize, and distribute knowledge throughout the organization.[2]

Generating content involves identifying content that might be relevant to others in the organization and then getting people to submit the relevant material to an electronic database. Most organizations have to go through a cultural change to shift the employee mindset from one of hoarding knowledge to one of sharing ideas. Steve Kerr, chief learning officer at Goldman Sachs & Co. and former chief learning officer at General Electric (GE), has noted that a prime component of former CEO Jack Welch's management system was to break down the barriers—both vertical and horizontal—across the organization so that knowledge transfer could occur.[3]

Many organizations spend significant sums on formal knowledge management systems. These systems must provide easy access to users. A "push" system catalogs the needs of users and selectively distributes information, often via e-mail, when it recognizes its potential value to a user. While this proactive approach can be somewhat obtrusive, it also recognizes that most employees are too preoccupied with their immediate tasks to take the time to search for existing company information that might be relevant and valuable to those very activities.

Knowledge management systems generally consist of:

- Databases and database management systems that collect and store the knowledge base.

- Communication and messaging systems that retrieve and transmit the material.

- A secure browsing feature that allows employees to search databases remotely, even from public access facilities, while protecting against unauthorized use.

The challenge is to find ways to motivate individuals to document their ideas and knowledge so that they can be available to others. The simplicity of this thought is belied by its difficulty to implement. Yet this difficulty did not dissuade most organizations in our BSC research database from identifying teamwork and knowledge sharing as a strategic priority in the learning and growth perspective of their BSCs.

Figure 2 shows representative examples of the objectives and measures for best-practice knowledge sharing. Organization G, a chemical company, monitors the number of best-practice ideas that are identified and used. It also measures output per employee to assess the economic impact from knowledge sharing. Organization H, a mutual insurance company, uses its corporate university to transfer knowledge. It measures the number of hours of training received by each individual. Financial services company I monitors the percentage of employees who transfer knowledge in a "work-out" process, patterned after the one created by Kerr and a team at GE.[4] Pharmaceutical company J and software company K use formalized knowledge management systems to transfer knowledge, and measure the level of system usage. Company K also monitors how up to date the material in its knowledge management system is. Financial services company L focuses on the comprehensiveness and currency of information in its performance databases. Rather than measuring the movement of ideas across the organization, manufacturing company M tracks the movement of key people who carry ideas, measuring the number of cross-divisional personnel assignments.

Organizations G through M in *Figure 2* measure knowledge sharing with input or process measures, not output or outcome measures, which are preferable. Either these organizations deem it too difficult to measure the outputs of knowledge sharing or they believe that these outputs show up in the form of improved performance elsewhere in their strategy maps. It seems, however, that organizations could do better at measuring outputs, using such metrics as "the number of new ideas transferred or adopted" or "the number of new ideas and practices shared with other teams and organizational units." Jack Welch, famous for making learning an organizational priority at GE, would question division heads about new ideas they had adopted from other GE units and new ideas that had originated within their units that they shared during the year with other GE units. Such questioning, backed up by actual performance measures, powerfully reinforces a culture of teamwork and knowledge sharing.

Organizational Capital: A Summary

The learning and growth perspective is the foundation of every organization's strategy. The measures in this perspective are the ultimate lead indicators; they represent the organization's intangible assets, which create value by their alignment to the organization's strategy. That is why only the Balanced Scorecard, not financial measures, can quantify the value that intangible assets create.

Human capital is enhanced when development investments are concentrated in the relatively few strategic job families that implement the processes most critical to the organization's strategy. Information capital is most valuable when it provides the vital infrastructure and strategic applications that complement human capital in promoting outstanding performance in strategic internal processes. The even more intangible organization capital—culture, leadership, alignment, and teamwork—is equally vital for successful strategy implementation. Organizations introducing a new value proposition must create a culture of customer-centric values. The transformation to the new strategy requires exceptional leadership throughout the organization. The new directions for the organization require that communication and performance management systems be aligned to what the organization wants to accomplish. Teamwork, in the form of information and knowledge sharing, is essential. The organization change agenda defines the target of this focus and alignment.

Some shy away from measuring these intangible assets—human capital, information capital, and organization capital—because by their very nature the measures will be "softer," or more subjective, than the financial measures conventionally used to assess organizational performance. The Balanced Scorecard movement has encouraged organizations to address this measurement challenge. Companies can now measure what they want, rather than wanting only what they can currently measure. And they've learned that just the simple act of attempting to measure the capabilities of employees, knowledge systems, and organization capital, no matter how imprecise, communicates the importance of these drivers in the value-creation process. The approaches described in this article illustrate how organizations have developed new ways to measure, and subsequently to create, their organization capital, thus stimulating the behavioral changes needed to become a successful Strategy-Focused Organization.

Notes

1. Peter M. Senge, *The Fifth Discipline: The Art and Practice of the Learning Organization* (Doubleday/Currency, 1990).

2. The content on knowledge management processes has been drawn from D. Garvin and A. March, "A Note on Knowledge Management," Harvard Business School Teaching Note #396-031 (November 1997).

3. S. Kerr, "Transformational Leadership: Lessons in Mastering Change at General Electric," presentation at the Balanced Scorecard Collaborative North American Summit (October 2002).

4. The GE Work-Out, widely documented, is a methodology that fosters knowledge sharing and organizational problem solving among employees up, down, and across organizational levels.

For Further Reading

"Measuring the Contribution of Human Capital" by David P. Norton (*Balanced Scorecard Report*, July–August 2001).

"Managing the Development of Human Capital" by David P. Norton (*Balanced Scorecard Report*, September–October 2001).

"Managing Strategy Is Managing Change" by David P. Norton (*Balanced Scorecard Report*, January–February 2002).

"Tear Down These Walls! How to Leverage Intellectual Capital" by Dr. Steven Kerr (*Balanced Scorecard Report*, July–August 2002).

Reprint B0403A

Addressing Major Obstacles to Change

• • •

The obstacles to organizational change are legion—and effective managers know how to identify and remove them. In the selections that follow, you'll discover strategies for driving change without triggering burnout and chaos, and for combating the exhaustion that can afflict employees in companies undergoing relentless transformation. Additional articles show you how to help employees move past fear of change, how to drive change initiatives that boost your company's profitability while also building long-term adaptability, and how to prepare for change long before the need for it reaches a crisis point.

Debriefing Eric Abrahamson

The Road to Better Recombination

• • •

Lauren Keller Johnson

You've heard the mandate "Change or perish!"—and you know it's true. So why are many companies changing *and* perishing? Simple—they've taken the mandate too far. Assuming that successful change requires total reinvention, managers have triggered excruciating cycles of initiative overload, chaos, and employee burnout. To reverse these cycles, Columbia Business School management professor Eric Abrahamson contends, we must change how we change.

Specifically, we need to augment the ever-popular "creative destruction" (which *is* sometimes necessary and useful) with what Abrahamson calls "creative recombination." Through creative recombination, managers reconfigure their companies' existing assets: people, structures, culture, processes, and networks. The payoff? Faster, cheaper, painless, and *sustainable* transformation.

Review Your Recombinants

Many companies have surprisingly rich supplies of assets, or "recombinants." These come in many forms:

- PEOPLE: Employees' knowledge, aptitudes, skills, social networks, values, and personal traits

- STRUCTURES: Divisions, departments, and units; lines of communication across functions and up and down the reporting hierarchy; and staffing and control mechanisms

- CULTURE: A company's values, norms, and informal leadership roles

- PROCESSES: The means by which a company purchases labor, materials, capital, and knowledge; turns these inputs into products and services; and brings its offerings to customers

- NETWORKS: Clusters (e.g., members of a department), cliques (e.g., small work teams), and hubs (people with connections across clusters and cliques)

Clone, Customize, Translate

You've got several ways of reconfiguring assets. Through *cloning*, you copy or revive a recombinant and use it in a different part of your business. With *customizing*, you alter certain recombinants so that they fit in different areas of your organization. And by *translating*, you reinvent recombinants to render them useful in an entirely new situation.

What do these techniques look like in action? Consider Westland Helicopters, a division of AgustaWestland, the largest division of London-based GKN Aerospace. After the Cold War ended, Abrahamson explains in *Change Without Pain*, Westland Helicopters "came under intense pressure to achieve economies of scale in development and production." Executives launched a dizzying round of initiatives that left the organization reeling. Eventually recognizing the signs of "repetitive-change syndrome," they decided to try a new approach to change.

"By looking around the division and its parent company to see what they already had in place," Abrahamson writes, "the executives found an easy, cost-efficient solution." They spotted an impressive product-development model in the company's in-house software division and adapted it to helicopter production, minimizing product-design costs. They also leveraged the knowledge of employees who had come to the division from the parent company's automotive sector and who had experience with mass-producing cars. Finally, they borrowed a product proposition that another division had long used. The so-called Barbie Doll model "enabled them to build a base helicopter that could be dressed up or recombined with any number of accessories-guns, bombs, avionics." Results? Mass production *and* mass customization.

To achieve this, Westland used all three creative-recombination methods. They *cloned* by reviving a long-lost value, a tradition of self-reliance that had gone into hiding during relentless change. They *customized* by adapting automotive experts' mass-production knowledge to helicopter production. And they *translated* by applying the functions served by each step in software development—not the steps themselves—to helicopter development.

Become a Better Recombiner

Westland Helicopters' story is remarkable; it's also rare. That's because many organizations misunderstand or misapply creative recombination. Abrahamson offers these guidelines for becoming a better recombiner:

Think "Both/And," Not "Either/Or"

"Don't assume you have to use *either* creative destruction *or* creative recombination," Abrahamson advises. "Sometimes you need a blend." Creative recombination is not a panacea—it's a tool that companies should add to their change-management repertoires.

The key? Knowing when to use which approach—or a hybrid of both. Creative destruction can shock a "change avoider"—a stable company with a limited variety of recombinants—into making the changes it needs to survive. But companies staggering from relentless reinvention may benefit more from creative recombination than another round of obliteration and rebuilding. Executives must nurture their company's capacity for *survivable* ongoing change. That can require what Abrahamson calls pacing: alternating periods of change (through creative destruction or recombination) with periods of stability during which a business can recover.

Use the Right Technique with the Right Recombinants

In addition to knowing when to use destruction and/or recombination, executives have to know when to clone, customize, and translate which recombinants. In his book, Abrahamson recommends looking for recombinants that lend themselves more readily to one technique than to another, depending on your circumstances.

For example, Sony cloned a product-return process it spotted in one of its network companies. Since the two companies were identical in all respects except for their return processes, it was clear how the cloned process would interface with existing processes.

Abrahamson writes that the company "plugged" the cloned process easily into its existing process flow and "let it play its role. Virtually no customization was necessary."

Some additional rules of thumb: Don't attempt to reconfigure lots of disparate recombinants at once—the resulting entities may prove unmanageably complex. And do think of creative recombination as a mosaic of focused changes you make over a period of time, rather than a linear series of discrete changes.

Use a New Vocabulary to Talk About Change

Creative recombination works best when a company's top leaders publicly advocate and model it. As Abrahamson notes, this active support requires that executives use a new vocabulary while talking about change with both internal stakeholders (managers, employees) and outside stakeholders (suppliers, customers, investors). "Creative destruction," he explains, "is so ingrained in business culture—especially in the West—that a leader who takes a creative-recombination approach may be perceived as doing nothing at all."

To counter such perceptions, executives must "tell different stories about change to people inside and outside the company." In conversations and statements, cite examples of the valuable recombinants residing in your company. Describe how your people are *already* reconfiguring them to generate desired results. Talk about how other companies are successfully using creative recombination, too. And introduce the notion of managing *stability,* not managing change. At the same time, contrast those examples with stories about destructive change your company has endured and point out its disadvantages.

Also look for audiences—such as layoff survivors—who may already be receptive to the idea of creative recombination because they've endured the scourges of destructive change firsthand. Leverage that receptivity by explaining the benefits of a different approach to change.

Be or Hire a "Chief Memory Officer"

To reconfigure existing assets, Abrahamson writes, you need to assess visible recombinants as well as assets lying "forgotten in your corporate basement." Look around your company for people who have the wisdom to "delve into the organization's past and revive old assets in order to craft new ways of solving pressing business problems."

Hired guns can write your company's history. But "remember that long-tenured employees are [your] best historians." These "memory keepers," Abrahamson writes, can "look back over past projects . . . before any 'innovation' is launched or *re*launched." And remember, "not all things a company did in the past are wonderful. . . . To avoid repeating mistakes, memory keepers should also [look] back into the firm's history to see whether a proposed change was attempted previously and what its outcome was and why."

Encourage "Messes, Messiness, and Messing Up"

A degree of chaos—for example, disorderly workspaces that put unrelated people and objects in surprising configurations—can lead to more effective creative recombination. Why? According to Abrahamson, messes throw people with "completely different knowledge and skills in close proximity so that they may learn from each other and find lucky recombinations of their varied expertise." And mistakes, while causing some damage, often yield new insights that turn out to be valuable when applied to a different situation.

Reprint U0402E

How to Overcome "Change Fatigue"

• • •

Nick Morgan

Chances are you've got a story like Andrea Zintz's. Now president of Andrea Zintz & Associates, a consulting firm, she was working for a health-care concern in 1997 when the firm's executive committee decided to launch an innovation initiative for 800 managers across all of its operating companies. Two weeks after the kickoff event—three fabulous days of inspirational talks by inventors, creators, and consultants—each attendee received a big box with the words "Tool Kit" on the front. It was filled with binders, pamphlets, videotapes, all kinds of useful information—and it sat on managers' shelves. No follow-up ever took place.

You're probably laughing—or wincing—in recognition of what has become a familiar tale of corporate change efforts. Indeed, with all the transformation efforts going on these days, the workplace seems to have transmogrified into one continual change initiative. Maybe it's a relief to know that only a few of these efforts will actually be carried through to completion, but that knowledge doesn't do much for morale. *Change fatigue* is rampant, and it's exacerbated by a natural tendency to distrust change that is imposed from above.

The remedy, say the experts, flies in the face of the revolutionary approach to change that reigned during the dot-com era's heyday: Pare down the number of initiatives. Be less preoccupied with large-scale transformation, and focus instead on small improvements. Above all, lose the notion that you need heroic leaders in order to have meaningful, sustained change.

Why Change Efforts Fail

"Change is one of the few areas where experts have been in violent agreement for decades," declares David A. Garvin, professor at Harvard Business School and author of nine books, including *Learning in Action*. The details vary, but in the main, all organizational change involves three phases: an initial stage of recognition and preparation, followed by the implementation of the actual changes and, finally, a period of consolidation. These phases are not linear, Garvin emphasizes: all three must take place for the change to work, but not necessarily in the order just described. Moreover, for each stage to be even marginally successful, certain conditions must be met.

In the first stage, the organization must evince widespread dissatisfaction with the status quo. Someone must develop a vision for the future and a plan to get there. During the second stage, there must be a real willingness to take on the resisters—the most dangerous of these, warns consultant Mike Hammer, are the ones who give you "the kiss of yes." The consolidation phase is the time for measurement and rewards. The organization must be ready to make changes to the change plan, based on an honest assessment of what's working and what isn't. It is at these moments that the flexibility of an organization is put to the test.

Change efforts fail for two main reasons, says Garvin:

Poor Design

These include the failure to address the underlying processes used to get the work done (for example, the performance management system, or the way resources are allocated), relying on IT to provide the magic bullet, and not explicitly tackling the necessary behavioral changes.

The Three Stages of Change

Stage I: The organization articulates the challenges that are motivating it to change. It designs a response and establishes goals.

Stage II: The actual change takes place. It's in the details of this stage that the proverbial devil lurks. This stage is one of execution and adjustment to hard, practical realities.

Stage III: The organization reviews what it has won and lost. This stage is about acceptance of limitations and adjustment to the new realities of the post-change world.

Poor Communication

A change initiative is like the start of a marathon: change will be occurring rapidly in some units, whereas in others it won't even have gotten under way. Change leaders need to be prepared to give the same speech at least six times or it won't get heard. Unclear intent is another problem. A change effort at Xerox foundered amid mutual recrimination and finger-pointing when an economic downturn revealed a lack of clarity about who was really in charge. Change leaders must explain the particular initiative thoroughly, letting employees hear the arguments for and against the options that were rejected. In addition, they must address employees' fears: "People want to know why you think they can make it through the change," Garvin observes. "They also want to know how you're going to help them through it."

Meaningful change isn't easy, but you don't have to be omniscient to pull it off, Garvin insists. Like a 19th-century Mississippi riverboat captain steering his boat from one bend in the river to the next, you just need to rely on point-to-point navigation.

Putting Lipstick on a Bulldog

Not only are know-it-all leaders unnecessary for successful change, they often muck it up. Echoing Garvin, Rosabeth Moss Kanter notes that it's very difficult for leaders to spell out in advance precisely what the future state should look like—so many who try merely get it wrong. A good leader uses a humbler approach that Kanter calls IKIWISI (I'll know it when I see it). She compares it to improvisational theatre: you make the best judgment you can in the moment and remain prepared to adjust to whatever new conditions arise.

"Personally, I hate change," acknowledges Kanter, Ernest L. Arbuckle Professor of Business Administration at Harvard Business School and author of 15 books, including *Evolve!*. "But I love renovating my house." Her point: nobody likes change when it's something that's done to us. But change that we think up or embrace on our own is different—*that* kind of change we never grow tired of.

Kanter likens the typical change effort to "putting lipstick on a bulldog." Here, the business leader sees something that's ugly, such as a process or a product that needs improvement. The leader wrestles with the change, and finding it difficult to get the thing to behave properly, decides just to make it look superficially better and move on. And the typical result of this misguided cosmetic effort? The bulldog's "appearance hasn't improved, but now it's really angry," says Kanter. Instead, she claims, "the key to substantive improvement lies in creating an environment in which employees don't even know that they're changing." Ricardo Semler, president of Semco, a privately held manufacturing and services company in São Paulo, Brazil, heartily agrees: by giving up the need to be in constant control, management allows change to happen on its own. Such a formula, he believes, has enabled his company to eliminate the "boarding-school issues" that take up 20% to 30% of managers' time—and that many formal change programs are designed to address.

Often described as "the world's most unusual company," Semco epitomizes the bottom-up approach to change. Employees choose their jobs, titles, places and hours of work, and even pay. Everyone in the company has a 360-degree evaluation every six months; these evaluations form the core of any needed change. Leaders are picked by their subordinates, and almost always come from within the company, so that no radical changes are imposed by new leaders from the outside trying to make a good impression. The CEO's position changes continually: four people regularly rotate through the job every year. The company doesn't even try to do annual budgets—six months is as far down the road as it can see. In short, Semco redefines change: instead of being the work of senior leaders, it's the responsibility of what Semler calls "atoms," groups of 8–12 employees who see to the company's basic processes. As a result, change becomes continual, gradual, low-level—and virtually unnoticed.

Kill the Hero, Save the Change

The applicability of Semco's model to large corporations is a matter of some debate. Nevertheless, Henry Mintzberg, a professor of management studies at McGill University, finds Semler's views well worth emulating. They're so refreshing, he says, because they run counter to most companies' tendency to overmanage; they manifest "the brilliance of knowing when to lay off." The notion that "change comes from the top," Mintzberg declares, is a fallacy "driven by ego," the "cult of heroic management," and the peculiarly American overemphasis on taking action. If companies in fact depended on dramatic, top-down change, few would survive. Instead, most organizations succeed because of the small change efforts that begin at the middle or bottom of the company and are only belatedly recognized as successful by senior management.

Enron, with its "loose-tight" management policy, is an example of an organization that figured out how to effect change without the usual pitfalls, says Mintzberg. The Houston-based energy company managed only two corporate processes very tightly: performance evaluation and risk management. Everything else was managed loosely, and local leaders got an enormous amount of discretion in figuring out how to get things done.

Mintzberg argues that the best kind of leader doesn't try to effect much change. Rather, she functions like a queen bee, which "does nothing but make babies and exude a chemical that keeps everything together." It is the other bees that busy themselves in going out to sense the environment, find sources of sustenance for the hive, and make the changes necessary to keep the hive alive in the face of an evolving environment.

To a certain extent, the media hype of the dot-com era required that leaders present a heroic face to the capital markets. Here's one reason to be thankful that the bubble has burst: no longer obsessed with the need for larger-than-life leaders and their grand strategies, we can now focus on a quieter, more evolutionary approach to change, one that relies on employee motivation instead of directives from on high.

For Further Reading

Learning in Action: A Guide to Putting the Learning Organization to Work by David A. Garvin (2000, Harvard Business School Press).

"How We Went Digital Without a Strategy" by Ricardo Semler (*Harvard Business Review*, September–October 2000).

"How Does Change Management Need to Change?" (*Harvard Management Update*, January 2001).

Reprint U0107A

So They Do More Than Survive

How to Help Your Employees When Roles Shift

• • •

Sharon Drew Morgen

There is a new urgency today around conversations about change. Because of reorganizations, downsizing, and shifts in product groups, employees at every level are being told that their jobs have been redefined and that they need to work better with fewer resources—or else.

But in rushing to the stark bottom line of these conversations, managers may overlook how much fear and resistance surrounds such change. This can be a big mistake, one that can cost them their top talent and leave their unit in chaos.

So how can you help your employees not just survive the change process but emerge from it better off? How can you help them continue operating as a team and support the change—and one another—through hard times?

It comes down to shifting the frame—to changing the change conversation. By using a process built around facilitative questions, managers can work with employees to uncover and address the sources of their resistance: their beliefs, presuppositions, and fears. These questions work to repattern thinking and align individual and team efforts behind the new processes or goals. Before opening these conversations with employees, though, managers need to consider why change is so difficult.

Change Challenges How Employees Define Themselves

Sales reps at a large insurance company were accustomed to making personal calls to seek new accounts, a costly procedure. So the company hired a consultant to train the sales force to use the phone as the initial method of contact and to visit customers only when they were ready to close. Sales skyrocketed!

But the reps revolted. Why? Because the dramatic shift in their daily routine challenged how they saw themselves. All of a sudden, they were in the office more than they wanted to be ("We're *field* reps," they said), they were on the phone more than they were used to ("We're *not* telemarketers," they said), and they were being coached more than they wanted ("We don't *need* micromanagement," they protested).

Change Creates Uncertainty

In the new work environment, your employees may lose status or have to work with someone they dislike—who knows? They certainly don't, and therein lies the problem.

Many managers feel they don't have the time or the skills to talk one-on-one with their employees about their fears—or they're afraid to. Yet, says Terah Stearns, president of Strategic Transformation, "this is a wonderful opportunity for managers to become leaders. They need to help their staff embrace the change, communicate any grief around the change, and find those people who have withdrawn into fear."

To bring employees' concerns out into the open and help employees address those concerns, managers can structure individual sessions or team meetings around the following question categories:

Discovering What's Missing

These questions help employees recognize what is different or difficult for them as the change process proceeds.

What do you like best about our current environment? What do you expect to see happening differently as this change progresses? How do you see that affecting you? Your job? Your relationships with your peers? Your results? At what point will it feel like you are being asked to make more changes than you'd prefer to?

How do you see yourself within the team as an employee? As a person? How do you see this shifting as a result of the change? If your role or relationships change to the point of being untenable, how will you seek support to alleviate the problems? What would you need to see from the team to work effectively, rather than leave the job or remain unhappy?

Making Internal Adjustments

Once employees realize the critical role they play as part of the team and part of the culture, they need to understand their responsibility to make personal changes.

What about this change do you see as being positive? Negative? What will you need to know or understand differently in order to accept those parts of the change that you currently are not comfortable with?

What skills do you already possess that will help you through this change? How do you propose getting any needed skills that you lack? What would you need from the management to support you through any relearning that you might have to do?

At what point will you recognize that you are having difficulty handling your internal issues on your own? What would be happening in your own behavior that you might want to check out? How could you use your teammates to help you?

Aligning Needs

Failure to align individuals' needs with those of the company will result in the loss of group cooperation and cohesion.

What beliefs held by the team need to be upheld during this process? Once all the people on the team have recognized how their needs and the company's are integrated, how will you recognize that the team is functioning optimally? Is there a need for more work on team dynamics and buy-in?

What would you see as warning signs that the change was creating a crisis in your work environment? Your work output? What actions would you be willing to take to enable others in your team to avert crisis? What skills would you need to learn in order to take responsibility to assist the team?

How could you support the entire team's learning and change process to grow into a more mature, skilled team with additional possibilities?

Making It Real

These conversations should become the basis for a series of group meetings or, better yet, a retreat or off-site devoted to discussion and decision making.

How do teams decide to take action? What needs to happen for this group to implement these ideas? How will the group recognize trouble? Fix the problem? Get help? What personal issues come up as the change nears completion?

Collaboration, Integration

When a team comes up with solutions, management has to show that it is listening to these ideas and willing to implement them. Ideally, the management team will use the facilitative questioning process to decide how to do so.

Change is unsettling, there's no doubt. The most efficient way to make it a positive experience for the team and the company is to make sure that each person is seen, heard, and taken into account. By bringing everyone into the equation, the odds are good that the change will be for the better.

Reprint C0212A

How Does Change Management Need to Change?

• • •

Leading change has become such an important managerial responsibility that each year entire forests are sacrificed to produce books on change management. The trend is likely to persist as long as the failure rate for change initiatives—two out of every three, report Harvard Business School professors Michael Beer and Nitin Nohria in *Breaking the Code of Change*—continues unabated. Many of these books offer similar advice, so they're often better skimmed than read cover to cover. But the best of them highlight an aspect of change initiatives in a way that grabs your attention.

Recommendations

Accept the fact that change is nonlinear.

As a living system, a business often changes in ways that cannot be predicted or controlled, argue Richard Pascale, Mark Millemann, and Linda Gioja in *Surfing the Edge of Chaos*. Instead of imposing an elaborately engineered solution onto a problem, disturb the equilibrium "in a manner that approximates the desired outcome," making mid-course corrections as the outcome unfolds. In the mid-1990s, Royal Dutch/Shell faced a competitive crisis: it had excess refining capacity, its cost structures were bloated, and it was losing market share to hypermarkets such as Wal-Mart that were selling fuel and lubricants at a loss. Steven Miller, managing director of Shell's Oil Products Business Committee, met these challenges by designing an approach that left ample room for improvisation. Rather than dictate the answers to Shell's operating company chairmen, Miller helped these influential executives discover how best to be connected to front-line operations.

Involve more people in the process.

In the current change management paradigm, the process of change is overseen by a "parallel organization," observes Richard Axelrod in *Terms of Engagement*. Composed of a sponsor team, a steering team, and a design team, this parallel organization can include a hundred or more people—from all levels and functions of the company. But even that level of representation is insufficient, especially for companies with upwards of 10,000 employees, Axelrod maintains—it constitutes the few deciding for the many. The result is increased employee resistance and a change plan lacking in essential "system knowledge" (ground-level understanding about how effective processes and relationships are built). Hewlett-Packard's microelectronics division successfully turned its five separate units into an integrated manufacturing organization by literally engaging the entire workforce. All 300-400 employees in the division attended a series of working conferences that overhauled the vision, customer-relationship philosophy, organizational structure, and technical processes.

Pay closer attention to the pockets of resistance.

In *Making Change Happen One Person at a Time,* Charles Bishop provides a model for identifying and responding to four types of employees: those who thrive in pivotal change positions, those who are supportive of change and willing to take on some new challenges, those who are uncomfortable with change but who are solid performers nevertheless, and those whose resistance is so strong that the company may be better off without them. How should you deal with these various groups? "Cure the wounded," advises Michael Mercer in

Absolutely Fabulous Organizational Change: help the employees "who sincerely want to help the organization improve, grow, and prosper." But "shoot the dissenters"—that is, "de-employ" those who refuse to get on the bandwagon.

All this advice is useful but piecemeal. Lacking an organizing framework that clarifies the reasons for a change initiative, the individual recommendations run the risk of being self-canceling. Here is where *Breaking the Code of Change* provides an invaluable service. This anthology of scholarly articles distills all change initiatives into two basic types—Theory E and Theory O—each of which has distinct advantages and shortcomings.

Theory E and Theory O

The singular focus underlying Theory E is the creation of economic value, often expressed as increased shareholder value. The various steps of the change plan are crafted and monitored from above and carefully laid out in advance. As Beer and Nohria point out, Theory E leaders focus on strategies, structures, and systems—the "hardware" of the organization—because these are "the elements that can be readily changed from the top down to yield quick financial results." Financial targets tend to dominate the agenda, and financial incentives are regularly used as drivers of the change—to align the interests of management with those of shareholders. Moreover,

Theory E leaders "often hire large consulting firms in multimillion-dollar engagements to bring in the motivation and knowledge employees are thought to lack."

Theory O isn't opposed to the creation of economic value—it simply maintains that creating sustainable competitive advantage is the best means of serving shareholders' long-term interests. The emphasis is not so much on short-term performance as it is on building organizational capability. This calls for a learning organization—an environment in which employees are emotionally committed to solving the new challenges that continually arise.

Theory E approaches are top-down, but Theory O approaches are characterized by high levels of participation. Instead of changing problematic structures and systems directly, Theory O efforts seek to change the culture that creates those structures and systems. And whereas Theory E initiatives are centrally planned and highly programmatic, Theory O approaches are more emergent—change percolates through the organization from the bottom up. Financial incentives serve to support the process of high involvement, not to drive it. And consultants are used in a more limited way: their role is not to provide answers but to set up a process by which employees make their own analysis and craft their own solutions.

Combining the Best of Both Theories

When your company or unit faces the need for major transformation, write Beer and Nohria, it's important to "avoid being drawn into an E *or* O approach without thinking through the ultimate long-term consequences." Moreover, the two approaches can be sequenced: General Electric's CEO Jack Welch followed up his Theory E approach—top-down plans for making every GE business achieve a number-one or number-two position in its industry—with Theory O initiatives such as the now-famous Workout process designed to create a boundaryless organization. Better still, say the authors, is "the simultaneous integration of Theories E and O," as exemplified by the efforts of Archie Norman and Allan Leighton to achieve improvements in shareholder value while also developing the organizational effectiveness of U.K. grocery chain Asda plc.

Much of the advice about improving change management ignores the fundamental tensions between Theory E and Theory O. The challenge, write Beer and Nohria, is to become exquisitely sensitive to these tensions—only then will you be able to discern ways of improving your change initiative that maximize the benefits and minimize the disadvantages of each theory.

For Further Reading

Breaking the Code of Change edited by Michael Beer and Nitin Nohria (2000, Harvard Business School Press).

Surfing the Edge of Chaos: The Laws of Nature and the New Laws of Business by Richard T. Pascale, Mark Millemann, and Linda Gioja (2000, Crown Business).

Terms of Engagement: Changing the Way We Change Organizations by Richard H. Axelrod (2000, Berrett-Koehler).

Making Change Happen One Person at a Time by Charles H. Bishop, Jr. (2000, AMACOM).

Absolutely Fabulous Organizational Change: Strategies for Success from America's Best-Run Companies by Michael W. Mercer, Ph.D. (2000, Castlegate Publishers).

Reprint U0101B

The Change Audit

A New Tool to Monitor Your
Biggest Organizational Challenge

• • •

Lila Booth

Four years ago, MTI, a manufacturer of motors and motor controls located in rural Minnesota, held an enviable reputation for products and service. The only problem: the company's main businesses were not aligned with changing customer preferences. MTI was, in the words of president Jim Folk, "a company not connected to technology, not connected to anything—even our *Wall Street Journal* arrived a day late." He can laugh now because MTI was subsequently able to adapt to the market changes and create an alternate future for itself;

indeed, within a four-year period, revenues doubled while staff increased by only 20%. But when Folk arrived in 1994, it was difficult to see much humor in the situation. "Our incoming order rate was declining at 10% to 15% per year for the four years before we adopted a culture of change," he remembers.

MTI's situation was hardly unique. In the '90s, the sea-swell of rapid, continuous change in markets, customer preferences, and technology threatened to capsize countless organizations. Issues related to corporate culture—specifically, does the culture embrace change?—were no longer "interesting" topics to think about when you had the time: they were matters of survival.

Change is the watchword of life, author Margaret Wheatley argues. It is "characteristic of living systems," she writes, "to continuously renew themselves." Borrowing insights from the natural world, her book *Leadership and the New Science* reads like Edmund Spenser's "Mutabilitie Cantos" for managers. Would that more consultants and business writers shared her deep sensitivity to the difficult psychology of change—many of these self-styled svengalis present a change process as little more than an oil-and-lube job. But if that were really the case, why are there so few examples of companies that have been able to institute and sustain large-scale changes or to create a culture that continues to welcome change? Change is, by its very nature, disequilibrating—even terrifying. It's completely understandable that a successful company would resist it, preferring to stick with proven formulas.

Understandable, but not good enough anymore. The best management thinkers tell us that the accelerating pace of change in today's economy means it's no longer enough to be responsive to *current* customer needs and competitive pressures. Companies must now look beyond their headlights to anticipate the changes ahead.

Given society's penchant for instant gratification, the time-consuming work of creating a culture adaptive to change can be massively frustrating. It often takes years, requires buy-in at all levels of the organization, and demands a deft and subtle managerial hand. Even on a smaller scale—when you're just trying to introduce a new product line, not transform the entire company's culture—change initiatives can be arduous. The hope behind these more modest initiatives is that they can add up to an overall climate that thrives on change—though undertaking the former is no guarantee that you'll end up with the latter.

In any such effort, whatever its scope, it's invaluable to have a tool to systematically monitor and manage what you're about. And here is one—the change audit, a structured way of ensuring that a change process maintains its momentum. Its most crucial components take place before and after the change process itself.

Before the change process begins . . .

Examine the history of response to change in your company.

If you don't understand the patterns of past reactions to change, you are doomed to repeat them. Knowing how change is perceived by employees illuminates the obstacles the process will face, which helps you plan ways of overcoming them. At MTI, this initial step revealed that the employees were extremely proud of their skills, and so interpreted the rethinking of the company's core business as an indictment of their basic worth.

Listen to a wide range of people, then build support among management and employees.

A change process must be participatory in order to succeed. People need a chance to express their assessment of the current situation, their hopes and anxieties about the process, their recommendations about how to proceed. Many companies handle this by bringing in an outside facilitator to conduct an assessment of what kinds of communication are needed. Meeting with small groups of employees, the outsider tends to be perceived as safe, and can therefore elicit more candid responses than a company facilitator. Only after thoroughly digesting these responses should the leader set about getting people to sign on to the change process she is contemplating.

With today's flatter organizational structures, negotiating change requires that management *throughout* the organization participate in the process as full partners. "In the emerging organization," Peter Drucker writes, "it has to be mutual understanding and responsibility." At MTI, Folk convened his senior management group with an outside consultant acting as facilitator, so that he could interact on a par with his managers, rather than as their boss. Together, the group agreed upon the direction in which the company needed to move. The president's sharing of responsibility for the effort enabled the senior managers' sense of initiative to come to the fore. It also made it easier for them to adopt an empowering approach in their own departments. In fact, the senior managers became the point persons for enlisting employee buy-in.

Getting buy-in is accomplished by giving employees reasons to perform to their full potential, which makes them more valuable to the company. The motivation can take a variety of forms. Joanne Carthey, founder of Net-Pro, a utility software producer in Phoenix, sees mutual respect as the cornerstone of any change effort. The company's four rules seek to capture the essence of its adaptive culture. "We make promises, we keep our word, we clean up our messes, and we have fun," she explains. Neutronics, an Exton, Pennsylvania instrument manufacturer, changed its reward system to foster the sense that everyone was in the battle together. "We took the top management and production people," notes CEO Terry Halpern, "and tied their compensation to gross profit—the thing employees could have control over. We also created an incentive program for engineering, based on the sale of new products."

Parse the anticipated risks and gains.

At MTI, it was fairly easy for Folk to convince people that the potential gains outweighed the associated risks. Maintaining the status quo meant a not-so-slow death; a fundamental rethinking of the business was clearly in order. At that embryonic stage of the process, building consensus around the need for change was more important than the details of what needed to be done differently. And not only did Folk portray change as essential, he also emphasized that it was *possible*; this optimism proved contagious.

The analysis of gains and risks won't always be clear-cut: the potential risks may be significant, requiring careful consideration that may steer your planning in more fruitful directions. But even if the risks are more than offset by the gains, the prospect of change may induce fear and cynicism in some employees—a sense of hopelessness or the feeling that the change process will require too much effort. In the early stages, before the precise strategy has been articulated, the leader's passion is often a crucial counterbalance to these emotions.

Decide on clear messages that need to be communicated.

What do you need to get across in order for the change process to succeed? At MTI, Folk and his senior managers mapped out a strategy to get the company where it needed to go, and then distilled it to its basic elements for ease of communication. It's essential to have the right people communicating the basic messages of the change process: it needs to be the people who have ownership in the process, who are willing to put themselves on the line for it, and who will be there providing support when things get rough. Also, plan in advance for how you will solicit and respond to feedback while the change process is ongoing. Folk and his senior managers took this a step further: they engaged in "contingency thinking," anticipating the issues that might impede progress and designing appropriate solutions in advance.

Create a time line for implementation and a set of performance measures.

"After clear change goals have been established," writes Timothy J. Galpin in *The Human Side of Change*, "the next step in implementing change is to measure performance against those goals." This is often the most difficult part of keeping a change process on track, because it means holding people accountable. At MTI, employees' performance is measured, in part, by the extent to which they are effective, innovative team members; performance expectations of managers include successful empowerment of others and team building.

Next, go about changing. As the change process proceeds and after it is complete, ask the following questions.

Has there been ongoing, effective communication during the process?

Don't assume you know what employees are thinking. Gather them in small groups; ask for *their* assessments, and if they find the process collaborative. It is often only at this stage that employees in companies with a history of top-down management begin to believe that their input is genuinely valued. Alternately, employees saying they feel locked out of the process indicates the need for collaborative skills training for company managers.

What stresses has the process created?

Treat stress as a diagnostic indicator. You have to know about its existence before you can find ways to channel it creatively.

What are the specific outcomes of the process?

This question keeps your company authentic—it pays to ask it continually throughout the effort. Look at each of the goals for the process. How much progress have you made? Is there any tweaking you can do now to improve performance?

Have successes been celebrated?

At NetPro, Carthey makes a point of celebrating as the achievements occur. Even a simple acknowledgment of success, she observes, can have "an amazing ripple effect."

What next?

"Even if you are on the right track," said Will Rogers, "you'll get run over if you just sit there." Asking this question helps build vigilance throughout the organization, write Sumantra Ghoshal and Christopher A. Bartlett in *The Individualized Corporation*. "Yesterday's winning formula quickly becomes today's conventional wisdom, and without vigilance, can eventually ossify into tomorrow's sacred cow."

Rust never sleeps. A change audit can help ensure that your company doesn't either.

For Further Reading

The Human Side of Change by Timothy J. Galpin (1996, Jossey-Bass).

The Individualized Corporation by Sumantra Ghoshal and Christopher A. Bartlett (1997, HarperCollins Publishers, Inc.).

Leadership and the New Science: Learning about Organization from an Orderly Universe by Margaret J. Wheatley (1992, Berrett-Koehler).

Managing in a Time of Great Change by Peter F. Drucker (1995, Truman Talley Books/Dutton).

Reprint U9803A

Driving Change Without a "Burning Platform"

. . .

You want your unit or organization to succeed—but success can make driving change even more difficult. Although *you* can clearly see that change will be essential in the future, your employees will likely be more skeptical. "Why do things differently, if we're already performing well?" they'll ask.

Success can breed complacency, and complacency is the enemy of any change initiative. As a manager, you need to apply special practices to drive change under these conditions. The articles in this section provide valuable guidelines and detailed examples of how managers and executives in successful companies have led change without a "burning platform."

Is Your Company a Prisoner of Its Own Success?

· · ·

Loren Gary

When Chuck Pilliod became president of Goodyear in 1972, he was convinced that his company was dangerously out of step with the latest technology for tires. Earlier, as head of Goodyear's International operations, Pilliod had watched Michelin grow to dominate the European market with its radial tire, which lasted twice as long, reduced the chances of blowout, and provided better fuel economy when compared to traditional bias tires like those Goodyear manufactured.

The signs were clear to Pilliod that the American market would likely follow suit. In fact, by 1972, Ford and

GM had already expressed their plans to use radials on all future models. Nevertheless, when Pilliod announced his goal of manufacturing 100,000 radial tires a day for the American market, he encountered heavy resistance. Salespeople didn't believe radials would sell because of the high cost, and several senior managers objected because the company's U.S. plants didn't have the right equipment.

Pilliod persisted, laying out an ambitious plan that involved combining U.S. and European R&D operations, applying world-class design ideas to the retooling of Goodyear's plants, and providing extensive training to all employees who would have a hand in the design and maintenance of the new equipment. The estimated bill: $2 billion.

Given this cost and scope, Pilliod knew that once Goodyear committed to manufacturing radials, there would be no going back. The company would be forever changed.

Pilliod's plan is a classic example of what Harvard Business School professor Donald N. Sull calls a *transforming commitment*, an action that increases the cost or eliminates the possibility of persisting in the status quo. Even though Goodyear was, at the time, the leading tire company in the U.S., Pilliod believed it was a mistake to maintain the current course. Goodyear had become a prisoner of its own success and was closing itself off to innovative ideas and strategies that would preserve its market leadership.

A transforming commitment doesn't require a brilliant strategic insight or a visionary leader. Its power derives from the ability of credible, clear, and courageous actions to harness organizational behavior and culture—that is, to bind managers to specific behaviors in the future. Not every company needs a transforming commitment, but those who find their core threatened often discover that it is the necessary lever for getting the organization out of the rut of familiar patterns of behavior. And although transforming commitments must come from the top of the company or business unit, middle managers can make vital contributions to the overall effort, says Sull.

Overcoming Active Inertia

Why do successful companies falter? Typically, it's not because their managers are paralyzed by some drastic shift in the environment (a change in technology, consumer preferences, or regulation), notes Sull in his new book, *Revival of the Fittest*. In fact, they tend to respond quickly. Nevertheless, the steps they take are ineffective because they exhibit *active inertia*, the tendency "to respond to even the most disruptive shifts in the environment by accelerating actions that worked in the past," writes Sull.

Over time, the distinctive success formula that helped a company beat out the competition can ossify. What were once insightful strategic perspectives become blinders. Innovative processes become mindless routines. And defining values turn into dogma. Instead of asking whether the logic that once made the formula successful still holds, company managers respond to market disruption by doing more of the same.

> What were once insightful strategic perspectives can become blinders.

Busting out of this prison calls for a powerful intervention. To appreciate just how powerful, it's useful to compare a transforming commitment with a similar concept: the catalytic mechanism. As noted management author Jim Collins explains in a *Harvard Business Review* article "Turning Goals into Results: The Power of Catalytic Mechanisms," a catalytic mechanism is a "galvanizing, nonbureaucratic means" of turning objectives into performance.

For example, Graniterock, a company that sells sand, concrete, and crushed gravel, adopted a short pay policy, which gave customers "complete discretionary power to decide whether and how much to pay based on their satisfaction level." An unhappy customer who doesn't feel that he should pay the full invoice has only to send the company a note explaining his frustration.

Such a policy "impels managers to relentlessly track down the root causes of problems," Collins writes. But as powerful as catalytic mechanisms are, not all of them go far enough to counteract the institutionalized inertia that success can breed. A transforming commitment, however, has a no-going-back aspect that undermines any attempt to continue with business as usual. Pilliod's approach—a public commitment to a stretch production goal—made it impossible for managers to sweep the matter under the rug.

A transforming commitment can take other forms as well:

Exiting a Business

In the early 1980s, British banks were suffering from defaults in their international loan portfolios at the same time that the British government was deregulating the banking industry. The managers at Lloyds' rival, National Westminster, "responded to these changes by accelerating their attempt to get big and diversify," Sull writes. But Lloyds CEO Sir Brian Pitman took a decidedly more radical approach. He closed the company's investment banking operation and exited global markets altogether in order to concentrate on its English customer base. In doing so, Pitman was able to make good on his pledge to double Lloyds' market capitalization every three years.

Betting the Farm on a New Direction

When Carlos Siffert was elected president of the Brazilian engineering firm Promon in 1989, he soon realized that the company couldn't continue to rely on state-sponsored infrastructure development projects for most of its income. The large internal work force that Promon used to staff these projects meant that profit margins were low, and the Brazilian government was on the verge of bankruptcy. Siffert describes his campaign to radically shift the firm's focus from consultating engineering to systems integration and project management as a "very visible and painful process" of downsizing the employee-owned firm to one-third of its 1986 level. By 1995, revenue per employee had surged by a factor of 15, and employee morale had grown steadily over that nine-year period.

Inviting Public Scrutiny

Lars Kolind, CEO of the Danish hearing-aid maker Oticon, revitalized the company by reworking its new product development process into cross-functional teams that "would assemble to develop a new product, collaborate for the duration of a project, and then disband," Sull writes. To buttress this change, Kolind publicly auctioned off Oticon's old hardwood furniture and bought new furniture with wheels "so that employees could roll their desks and files from one team to another." Then he let the Danish press televise Oticon's move to its new headquarters, an abandoned factory with no enclosed offices.

Actions such as these reinforce the credibility of the transforming commitment, showing employees that the manager "will stay the course even when changes in the business context might promote another course of action in the future," writes Sull.

Making the Commitment

Clarity is also critical for traction. Transforming commitments don't have to be revolutionary: There was nothing novel about CEO Lou Gerstner's shifting IBM's strategy from selling mainframes to selling integrated solutions. But they do need to "present a clear alternative to the established success formula," Sull writes. It also helps when you make the commitment simple and concrete, repeat it continually, and provide means for measuring progress.

Finally, a transforming commitment requires courage, which Sull defines as the willingness to break with the existing formula rather than fortify it, and the steadfastness to implement the commitment with a grinding consistency. For example, Pitman's pledge to double

Transforming commitments don't have to be revolutionary.

Lloyds' market capitalization every three years left no doubt about his moxie.

Of course, not all companies are in a situation that requires a transforming commitment. If the environmental change in your industry doesn't threaten your core business, or even if it does threaten your core but you have no viable alternative businesses to develop, then it probably makes the most sense to continue with your existing success formula, Sull advises. But if the changes do threaten your core and you do have a good alternative, that's when the strong medicine of a transforming commitment is most effective.

How do you get started? First, you need to choose an anchor, an overarching objective that will guide your subsequent actions. For some companies, the right anchor will be reframing the strategy. For others, it will mean renewing the resource base, introducing a completely new methodology such as taking on stretch relationships in which you promise a specific level of performance to key stakeholders.

And in rare instances, says Sull, you can energize employees by minting a new set of values, as McKinsey & Company's Marvin Bower did in the 1930s when he grafted professional norms of hiring and promoting staff characteristic of the fields of law and medicine onto a firm rooted in an accounting heritage.

Once you've settled on an anchor, you need to take steps to ensure that it's credible and well understood. From there, it's a matter of realigning the rest of the organization. Having a clear anchor can help you decide which challenges to tackle first. At IBM, revamping the sales force, which was organized by geography and lacked expertise in specific industries, became a high priority given Gerstner's new strategy of providing integrated solutions.

Although the discussion here has focused on CEOs' actions, if you're the head of a business unit or division, you're also in a position to make and implement transforming commitments. To succeed, you have to have sufficient autonomy (either geographical distance from headquarters or distance from the core business). Your commitment must be consistent with the broader corporate direction, and you need to be able to stay long enough to fulfill it. It also helps if you can fund the commitment without help from corporate.

As Sull describes in his book, George Mosonyi and Istvan Kapitany, the local managers of Royal Dutch/Shell's business in Hungary, achieved dramatic success when they committed to "increasing nonfuel revenues from the Shell Select gas stations with convenience stores" by turning the gas station managers into mini-CEOs with the power "to decide for themselves what to sell and what prices to charge." In 1991, Mosonyi and Kapitany's efforts increased nonfuel retail sales by 60%.

For Further Reading

Revival of the Fittest: Why Good Companies Go Bad and How Great Managers Remake Them by Donald N. Sull (2003, Harvard Business School Press).

Reprint U0308B

Debriefing
Richard Koppel

Change Without a Burning Platform

• • •

In 2002, Richard Koppel, GTECH Corporation's newly hired vice president of advanced technologies, faced a dilemma. The Rhode Island-based company—which creates and manages networked marketplaces primarily for lottery customers—had captured a 70% share of its market and seen its stock price skyrocket. GTECH was deftly handling as many as 500 million transactions daily and had achieved the industry record for system reliability. Each year, the firm was processing billions of dollars in transactions.

But Koppel knew there could be trouble ahead. Much of the 21-year-old company's legacy technology was

> Employees ask,
> "If we're doing so well, why
> in the world would we want
> to change anything?"

based on increasingly antiquated programming languages such as Fortran, while the majority of the IT world had moved on to Web-based technologies. "Our systems were old, inflexible, and highly proprietary," Koppel says. "I knew that even though we were doing well at the time, we'd have increasing trouble serving our customers in the future. Their needs were changing, and they wanted more Web- and Linux-based systems. We wouldn't be able to innovate quickly enough or affordably enough to meet those needs unless we started using newer technologies."

To remain competitive, Koppel knew that GTECH had to undertake a major change initiative, one that would drastically overhaul the company's technology platform. But while Koppel had the enthusiastic support of GTECH's executive team and a substantial financial commitment to fund the initiative, he encountered stiff resistance from the people charged with carrying it out. They simply couldn't see any rationale for initiating transformative and disruptive change at a time of unprecedented corporate achievement.

In companies enjoying high performance like GTECH, change leaders face unique challenges. Employees ask, "If we're doing so well, why in the world would we want to change anything?" And if managers do spot something that worries them—such as outdated technologies or processes that might pose problems way down the line—they often find it excruciatingly difficult to convince the workforce that those worries must be addressed now. After all, as John Kotter made clear in his book *Leading Change,* successful change leaders must take their organizations through a specific series of steps—starting with establishing a sense of urgency. Each step builds on the next. Thus, if there's no sense of urgency, managers can't move to the subsequent steps, such as creating a guiding coalition and developing and communicating a compelling vision.

Resistance to Koppel's initiative took various forms. Some engineers refused to attend the Web-based programming courses GTECH provided, claiming that they couldn't take time away from their jobs. Others discredited the new technologies. Yet despite the intensity of the resistance, Koppel eventually overcame employees' reluctance to adopt the new technologies. Today, GTECH wins new contracts even when it's not the lowest bidder. "After the Florida lottery selected us," Koppel explains, "they told us that we were 'light years ahead' of our competitors."

How did Koppel manage to drive profound change without an immediate crisis and achieve such admirable results? He applied five principles that he maintains are crucial to any company seeking to launch an "anticipatory versus reactive" change initiative:

1: Communicate and Educate Constantly

Make the business case for your initiative in irrefutable terms, and repeatedly communicate the importance of the program, just as if you were explaining it to someone outside the company. Koppel circulated among GTECH's mid-level and frontline managers and showed them how to explain to employees why the new program was crucial. "You have to phrase it as if you were trying to explain it to your grandmother," he asserts. In GTECH's case, Koppel expressed the perils of the company's situation in straightforward language: "We won't be able to serve our customers in the future." He and other managers also traveled to GTECH's international offices to visit the roughly 1,000 product-development employees who would be most affected by the change effort.

In addition, Koppel sent repeated messages about the need for change through every communication and educational channel possible. For example, he invited outside experts to conduct in-house "brown bag" lunches on the subject of the new technologies. He asked programmers from Sun Microsystems, Hewlett-Packard, IBM, and other firms to come speak "peer to peer" with GTECH's employees. E-mails, articles on the company's intranet, and regular staff meetings further turned up the volume. Koppel even instituted the "Pizza with Richard" lunch program, through which he personally hammered home the importance of change. The firm also developed streaming videos for the company's intranet that explained how employees would benefit from the change initiative. "We continue to do all these things even today," he says.

2: Set Your Vision, Then "Manage to It"

Demonstrate that you "mean business" and that you're committed to making the change happen. At GTECH, some people who had resisted the initiative were let go. But the company "wound in the pressure," Koppel explains, primarily by hiring numerous new employees who had the desired skills and attitudes. GTECH also established reward and recognition programs to encourage the right behaviors. For example, programmers who became certified in Java, a Web-based programming language, received companywide praise and monetary rewards. "The recognition set off a chain reaction," Koppel notes. "More and more people started attending the courses, and people got competitive about it."

But Koppel also advises knowing when not to push people. To illustrate, some of the most change-resistant employees were the only individuals who possessed the knowledge and expertise to service the older systems still functioning in GTECH's marketplace. The company needed those people—and the engineers knew it. "They're the best at what they do," says Koppel, "so we decided we could live with some level of resistance."

3: Set Boundary Conditions

Dictate the business requirements for the new ways of operating that will result from your change initiative—but let employees decide how they'll fulfill those requirements. For example, Koppel gave GTECH's programmers a list of the capabilities the new systems would need—such as the ability to integrate third-party software. Then he invited them to assess how well their current system met those requirements. "When they said, 'Our old technology doesn't do that,'" Koppel explains, "I asked them how they planned to meet the defined conditions. When you tell people what they need to do but let them figure out how it's going to get done or how to do their jobs, you get much better buy-in."

Koppel refers to chaos theory in discussing his approach to change management. "In complex, nonlinear, dynamic systems," he says, "order emerges out of chaos, and the details are unpredictable. You have to set the initial conditions for change and create the context. But then you provide minimum specifications—just a few hard rules, which people can figure out how they're going to follow."

4: Admit Your Mistakes

Probe for difficulties that employees may be encountering in making the transition. Acknowledge when you've made an error, and be willing to make midcourse corrections. In addition, accept the fact that major change involves a lot of uncertainty. Koppel had extensive expertise with the Web-based technologies he was proposing for GTECH, but he was new to lottery software. When an employee proved to him that third-party software Koppel had insisted on installing presented integration difficulties, Koppel willingly agreed to jettison the product—even though GTECH had already paid $1 million for the license to use it. "You have to make it safe for people to bring problems to you," he says. "Invite employees to talk about difficulties they're having, and don't punish them for pointing out mistakes you've made."

5: Adjust Your Leadership Style

Know when it's time to dictate and when it's time to use a more collaborative approach to leading change, focusing on how to most effectively set the conditions for success. "GTECH has a consensus culture," Koppel says, "so people don't take very well to someone dictating to them. I did have to make it clear that the change to the new technologies wasn't open to debate. But you can't implement a major change through command-and-control. You can't make people learn something they don't want to learn."

To persuade rather than force resistant employees to embrace change, Koppel "cautiously moved people into their discomfort zone" by explaining the specific consequences of not adopting the new technologies. "I told them that if we didn't make this change, we'd not only have problems satisfying our customers, we'd also find it harder and harder to comply with government procurement requirements," which can make or break a provider's chances of winning a contract. Arguments with that level of detail are tough to refute.

Reprint U0404E

If It Ain't Broke, Fix It Anyway

Communicating to Create Change at Ford

• • •

Betty A. Marton

Tony Zambito, a product design engineer at Ford Motor Company, had mixed feelings when he first learned about the company's plans to streamline and unify its worldwide operations. Heralded by *BusinessWeek* as "a massive overhaul that is shaking the 91-year-old company to its roots," Ford 2000 was first announced in April 1994 when Zambito had been at the company for nine years—not long enough to be as skeptical as some old-timers, but long enough to need convincing that this was good for the company and for him.

"I didn't know how to feel, it was so big," he says. "It took a long time to understand that this is consistent with what other successful companies are doing."

When Ford 2000 was first conceived, business was strong for the world's second largest automaker, with record earnings and revenues. But projected trends showed an inevitable competitive decline—unless the company did something drastically different. Ford realized it had to dramatically streamline its operation on many levels and bring down the cost of production worldwide. This was the message that was used to rouse employees who had no inclination to change familiar, and seemingly successful, ways of doing business.

"We had to let people know that although everything seemed fine, it wasn't," says Chuck Snearly, director of communication services. "We had to communicate a sense of danger and opportunity." Thus Ford 2000 was conceived to galvanize people to change successful habits.

Ford took its first steps toward restructuring the company's processes in January 1995, only eight months after the concept was introduced. From the very beginning it was proposed as a work-in-progress to employees, who were viewed by top executives as critical players in developing and executing the company's global realignment.

To this end, Ford developed a multi-pronged, multimedia communications program that was, and continues to be, a way not only to disseminate information, but to help promote change. Supported by accessible and open top executives, the company's in-house communications team produced an ongoing avalanche of print, video, and electronic media that gave employees the information they needed—both good and bad—consistently, frequently, and before they heard it from outside sources.

"If you're going to talk about news, you've got to be able to expose the warts," says Beryl Goldsweig, then manager of employee communications. "Our credibility was very important. We didn't want to become an internal public relations agency by saying that everything was always wonderful. We learned how to handle bad news without pointing fingers and to speak about failures within the context of eventual success."

Communication Flowing Uphill and Down

Brought together in a series of working meetings, Ford's top global executives and managers were expected to play an active role in spreading the gospel of Ford 2000. Information that came from the top was to be cascaded down the ranks in face-to-face meetings so that all employees heard what they needed to know in person from their supervisors.

Senior managers were encouraged to step outside of

their business units and, using talking points provided by corporate communications, exchange information cross-functionally with other employees. To reinforce the concept of cascading information down the hierarchy, corporate communications faxed a weekly publication, *Grapevine,* to the company's top 3,000 global managers. Along with confidential news and stories of how Ford 2000 was being implemented, *Grapevine* promoted the downward flow of information by publishing reports on what was being disseminated, and where and how changes were being handled.

"*Grapevine* indirectly put the pressure on managers to make sure they were cascading information down to the troops," says Snearly.

As Ford 2000 progressed, *Grapevine* went from a faxed sheet to an electronic publication. Now it's called *Insight,* and both its circulation and coverage have expanded, with information in local editions tailored to specific sites.

Leading by Example

In its efforts to promote frank and frequent communication, as well as to enable a two-way sharing of information, management led by example in a variety of ways. Now retired Chairman and CEO Alex Trotman traveled to Ford plants and office facilities around the world, holding face-to-face "town hall" meetings where he listened to questions and suggestions from employees.

The Lessons of Ford 2000
How to Foster Change When the Stakes Are Big

Make it real. Ford 2000 isn't just another corporate PR program. It's also creating real changes in the huge corporation.

Share the bad news along with the good. It's enormously important—and difficult for executives to agree to do—to get beyond corporate happy talk. If you're not prepared to be honest, don't start.

Tailor the message to the audience. Messages must be shaped for different audiences and different cultures. Look for local "hooks" that help bring a story to life for the plant in Düsseldorf, for example, and for the one in Dubuque.

Use all the available technology and media. Messages are reinforced and seem credible when they come to people from different sources. Workers may discount the value of stories they only read in the company newsletter, for example.

Learn from outsiders. Don't assume you have all the answers. Creative solutions may well come from your peers in a wide variety of other organizations.

Overcommunicate. Don't assume that because you've heard it, everyone else has. You must drive your message home relentlessly for a big corporation to "get it."

> Ford realized it had to dramatically streamline its operation on many levels and bring down the cost of production worldwide.

Twice yearly meetings from Ford's headquarters were also broadcast globally with open phone lines for call-in questions from employees.

Top executives also made themselves available on a weekly basis to answer employees' questions during hour-long, unrehearsed interviews on FCN-TV, Ford's in-house television network. Company reporters felt free to nab them for on-the-spot interviews.

"We tried to mix news with what people wanted to know and what they needed to know," says Sara Tatchio, who was executive producer of FCN-TV. "Our job was to overcommunicate, share everything, and make employees part of the team."

But the pace and the pressure of Ford 2000 often made it more difficult to get the story from managers who weren't sure where to draw the line of confidentiality.

"Very often we'd run into managers who were nervous

about sharing information," says Goldsweig. "There was a lot of back and forth to get approvals without letting them write the life out of a story. It sometimes meant going several steps up the totem pole so they could know that not only was it okay, but that it was important to allow this material to be published."

Getting It on Tape

In April 1994, when plans for the global realignment were first unveiled in Toronto to the top 350 executives, Tatchio was on hand to videotape the meeting. She and her colleagues stayed up all night editing the tape, which was shown at 8 a.m. the next day at the first meeting of 1,800 global managers who gathered in Orlando, FL. Excerpts were also prepared for Trotman's live 9 a.m. network announcement, which was fed to 350 locations around the world.

During the next two years, Tatchio's team produced more than 100 tapes, from meeting highlights to a five-minute overview of Ford 2000, all of which are available to all employees.

"Maybe it was overkill, but our overriding goal was to make sure employees knew all the news as quickly as possible, before anyone else," she says. "The energy from the top was so contagious and the philosophy was so different from what you would expect from corporate life. You heard the word 'yes' a lot. We never wanted to be seen as a propaganda tool, so we walked a fine line of asking people to review for accuracy, not for words and not letting any one person dictate how a story should run," she says. "The atmosphere of Ford 2000 made that more possible than ever."

Employees' support for Ford 2000 was gauged through surveys initially conducted every six weeks and then quarterly. The surveys also helped determine employee response to the barrage of information they were receiving, which also included *Ford World*, the company's monthly publication, and other local publications that were created to spread the Ford 2000 message.

The results of the survey were tallied by country and function and analyzed to determine the strengths and weaknesses of the communications program.

"Surveying was essential. You can't improve if you don't measure the results of what you are doing," says Goldsweig. "We kept track of what kind of support we were getting, what kind of face-to-face information employees received, and whether they heard their news from us, the outside media, or the rumor mill."

Different Ways to Deliver the Same Message

Cultural and language differences made it difficult to deliver consistent messages to employees, especially in countries such as Argentina, Brazil, and Venezuela, where

Ford had manufacturing sites but no communications vehicles. Mike Parris, manager for mass communications, worked closely with employees in Latin America and in Ford's Asia-Pacific plants to determine just how the messages of Ford 2000 should be delivered through monthly newspapers and teletext systems in the lunch rooms and break areas of plants.

"There are different ways to deliver the same message and we learned that we had to be flexible," he says. "It didn't make sense to feed straight stories, and we couldn't get into tons of approvals, so we would share themes and then trust them to do the job right."

To keep ideas flowing, members of the communications team benchmarked their operations with other companies and held off-site meetings with a facilitator to brainstorm ways of getting the messages out.

"It was difficult to find the time, but we'd do it—away from phones and meetings," says Lauren Sides, then communications manager. "It's important to take a step back and see what's working. No matter how many media venues you have, it still boils down to small targeted efforts."

The Big Payoff

Sides was responsible for developing an online version of FCN that was updated daily from both Dearborn and London with news and stock prices, and that by 1998 was receiving well over one million hits a month. FCN-TV is also now broadcast directly to the desks of all salaried employees.

"Use of the Intranet grew like wildfire and became our best, cheapest, and quickest global tool," she says.

A specific site for communicators has become the primary resource for creating and disseminating globally consistent information. Communicators from any Ford location in the world can download background information, high-resolution photographs, and country-specific product and marketing information for use in local publications and broadcasts.

Ford is still on the road to its goal of reducing the number of basic vehicle platforms by 50%, increasing the number of parts common to different vehicles, and providing more choices for customers. The company, which has nonetheless already reported reduced costs, increased productivity, profits, shareholder value, and market capitalization and improved quality, continues to push the messages and look for feedback about Ford 2000.

"The idea was and continues to be communicate, communicate, and communicate, until you get sick and tired of communicating," says David Scott, Ford's recently retired vice president of public affairs. "That's when people are only beginning to get the message."

Reprint C9905D

Communicating Effectively About Change

. . .

Effective communication is one of the most crucial tools in your change-leadership arsenal. In the articles that follow, you'll find a wealth of recommendations and tactics for conveying a sense of urgency around change, winning commitment to change, and sustaining momentum during difficult change initiatives.

For example, you'll see how presenting your message in many forms, including stories, pictures, statistics, and metaphors, can ensure that your employees understand your vision—the first step in driving change. And you'll find graphic examples of how to make your messages about change visible, and even touchable, for maximum impact. You'll also discover what kinds of information you need to convey to employees to drive successfully—and when to deliver the information.

Communicating Change

A Dozen Tips from the Experts

• • •

Rebecca M. Saunders

Change programs. All too often, they're neither one. They fail to effect change well, and they fail as systematic programs. Usually forgotten in the resulting chaos is the most critical group of all: the employees. Why is the record so bad? Lesson One: Don't rely on a "Big Bang" announcement to persuade employees to fall in line. It's never enough.

Nor are existing communication channels adequate to report progress. Such channels often break down in the highly emotional climate that surrounds a change program.

163

Employees are hungrier than ever for answers and information, says Price Pritchett, a change management expert at Pritchett & Associates. When they don't get the information they need, they turn to the rumor mill. Pritchett cites a study showing that 20% of an organization's employees tend to support a change from the start. The rest are either fence sitters (about 50%) or resisters whom nothing can sway (30%). It's this 80% to whom communications should be directed. William Bridges, author of *Managing Transitions: Making the Most of Change* and consultant to Fortune 500 companies, has found that often a change process meant to strengthen an organization actually weakens it by leaving people confused and resentful when management really needs their commitment. To prevent this, says Bridges, managers need to take pains to communicate effectively throughout the process. Bridges identifies two questions that managers need to ask about their communications:

- Am I giving as clear a picture as I can of the what, when, how, and why of the changes?

- Is it enough to rely on the old communication channels to give and receive messages, or do I need to create new channels?

Following are a dozen tips from the pros on how to make change work.

1: Specify the Nature of the Change

Slogans, themes, and phrases don't define what the change is expected to achieve, says Gary F. Grates, president and CEO of Boxenbaum Grates, Inc., a communications firm. Instead, communicate specific information about how the change will affect customer satisfaction, quality of product, market share or sales, or productivity. Says Grates, "Change must be seen in the context of a tangible goal, either on a corporate level—to become first or second in the industry; on a division level—to increase revenue by 20%; or on a department level—to shorten delivery time to two days."

2: Explain Why

Employees are often left in the dark about the business reasons behind corporate changes. Alan Brache, director of consulting services for Kepner-Tregoe, believes it's because the people announcing the change have spent so much time studying the facts that it never occurs to them that their employees don't know them. In addition to discussing what's prompting the change, managers should share with employees the various options considered and rejected before they came to the final decision, says Brache.

3: Let Employees Know the Scope of a Change Even If It's Bad News

Some changes may affect only a few individuals within the organization, while others may affect everyone. In either case, it's best to end speculation. While you may be tempted to sugarcoat news, don't. Joseph Gibbons, a consultant with William M. Mercer's New York office, advises: "If there will be layoffs, say so. If the company is selling off a division, let employees know." Gibbons recalls how management at one company felt it couldn't tell employees it was searching for a buyer because "morale would plummet." Morale plummeted anyway as the story seeped out. "The rumors were worse than the reality as employees speculated on buyers with histories of post-purchase layoffs."

4: Repeat, Repeat, and Repeat Again the Purpose of the Change and Actions Planned

If the initial announcement doesn't generate questions, do not assume that employees accept the need for change—it may only mean that the announcement came as a surprise, says Richard Worth, coauthor of *The Four Levers of Change*. Once employees are back at their desks, then they'll begin to worry, and that's when the communication process has to rev up. Follow up that first meeting with a second meeting, and that second meeting with a third, and so forth, to get a dialogue going with employees. "Employees can take bad news; they don't handle uncertainty as well," says T. J. Larkin, president of Larkin Communication Consulting and coauthor of *Communicating Change: Winning Employee Support for New Business Goals*. "Uncertainty can kill a company." Besides repetition, Larkin suggests dividing communications into "small chunks" so the plan is more easily understood.

5: Use Graphics

Hand-drawn pictures on a flip-chart or an overhead projector can simplify corporate restructures. Whether the new organization looks like a square, triangle, or a giant amoeba, the drawings can help employees visualize the new organization. When management at Sears, Roebuck & Co. was trying to reinvigorate the company, it utilized "learning maps" in small group meetings that showed retail-market trends to explain the company's need to change, according to Steven P. Kirn, VP of human resources planning and development.

6: Make Sure Communication Is Two-Way

Small, informal meetings on a local level enable managers to respond to employee concerns and to gauge the level of likely resistance within the organization. These interactions may unearth ways to make the change plan work better, says Brache, but such meetings don't commit management to anything more than listening to the employees and responding to their suggestions.

With front-line employees, Larkin decries huge meetings—he calls them the "big bang approach to communication." Instead, he advocates small group meetings in which you can truly talk to employees about the change. You also avoid the danger of fringe or hostile groups disrupting a large meeting.

Says Worth, "Change happens at the emotional level, not at the rational level. Informal meetings with employees can go a long way toward a change in heart as well as in head."

7: Target Supervisors

All the experts say supervisors should play a key role in corporate change plans, but Larkin goes a step further, suggesting supervisors should communicate the need and nature of the change from the start.

At an offshore oil company, Larkin recalls, supervisors attended half-hour briefing sessions prior to a major change in maintenance operations that would include layoffs. Supervisors were also asked about their concerns regarding the change. Their responses were compiled anonymously into an opinion report for the management team, which then tried to work as many of the recommendations into the plan as possible. The final plan was then shared with the supervisors, who were charged with explaining the change to their employees. Management also developed change booklets to guide face-to-face discussions between the supervisors and their employees.

8: Support Change With New Learning

When studies at Owens-Corning showed sales revenue could grow by changing the company's selling method to emphasize value and relationship, employees were offered training to build credibility in the new method, recalls John Mallin, leader of corporate learning and development. Mallin observes, "The training answered the question, 'Why should I change how I've been selling?' Elements of good learning include an awareness that you have to change, acceptance of that fact, commitment to the need to change, and fourth, and most important, teaching the appropriate skills to get to the right outcome."

9: Point to Real Progress

Grates recalls how Greg Brennemen, president and COO of Continental Airlines, found employees didn't believe that the firm's change efforts were meaningful until he could point to the fact that all the planes had been painted, the carpets had been replaced, and the lighting in terminals had been improved. Until then, it was only rhetoric to the employees.

10: Don't Limit Communications to Meetings and Print

As e-mail replaces paper as the main means of internal communications, some managers and employees won't even look at paper memos or reports. The urgency associated with e-mail increases the likelihood it will be read. At Owens-Corning, weekly e-mail messages from the CEO went to business leaders who forwarded the e-mail down through the organization. Another company created videos that ran continuously in the cafeteria. Says Gibbons, "If you ate, you heard it. Literally, the tapes gave employees facts, not false rumors, to chew on." A third organization distributed cassette tapes about its change efforts that managers and employees could play on their commute to and from work.

11: Institutionalize Information Flow about the Change

Mark Childers, senior vice president of organizational development and human resources at Champion International and coauthor of *What Works: A Decade of Change at Champion International,* points to a 10-year ongoing effort to keep a 100-plus-year-old company competitive. The company chose to approach the challenge in a systematic way. A companywide cross-functional team performed a thorough study of how information flowed through the organization. The group discovered that the individual mills didn't talk often with each other, which meant that there was no mutual learning. Meetings designed to share information got the communication started. But it really heated up when the best-practices participants were given laptop computers. "Operating people burned up cyberspace with their queries, shared experiences, and ideas." As the organization has moved to Lotus groupware, the opportunities for mutual learning have grown—and maximizing best practices has become an ongoing goal of manufacturing.

12: Model the Changes Yourself

"Managers who talk one way and behave another communicate much more than words," reminds Grates, who is also founder and chairman of the Institute for Excellence in Employee-Management Communications, a think tank on organizational effectiveness. "Too often companies in change efforts don't do a good enough job to see that their directives are consistent with their own actions. It's this that has spawned the *Dilbert* industry. As actions refute words, employees become frustrated and alienated. They stop hearing what management is saying because what it is doing speaks so much louder." Worth gets to the point: "Words and actions have to be consistent with the change strategy. Walk the walk, and talk the talk."

For Further Reading

Communicating Change: Winning Employee Support for New Business Goals by Sandar Larkin and T. J. Larkin (1994, McGraw-Hill).

The Four Levers of Change by Richard Worth and Peter L. Brill (1996, AMACOM).

Managing Transitions: Making the Most of Change by William Bridges (1991, Perseus Books).

What Works: A Decade of Change at Champion International by Richard Ault, Richard Walton, and Mark Childers (1998, Jossey-Bass).

Reprint C9908A

You're Ready for Top-Line Growth— Are Your Employees?

• • •

Angelia Herrin

As the vital signs of the U.S. economy continue to improve, many companies are starting to pay more attention to top-line growth and less to cost savings. But switching to an invest-and-grow mindset requires a different orientation from cost cutting and belt tightening, a change that will demand refocused attention and communication from leaders who want employees to approach priorities and resources in a new way, says William Bridges, consultant and author of the best-selling *Managing Transitions: Making the Most of Change.*

"It's not just a change in the company strategy, it's a change in the rules and a much deeper cut at habits and assumptions," says Bridges. "You can announce that you want investment and speed and growth, but you aren't going to get results unless you understand what is involved when you ask people to stop doing what has worked for the past few years and start doing something in a new way."

Managers can smooth and speed changes, Bridges says, by understanding that a successful transition needs the completion of three phases he calls the ending, the neutral zone, and the new beginning.

"Transition and change are not the same thing," says Bridges. "With change, you are focused on the outcome the change produces. But that change goes nowhere unless the leader can play a transitional role too. The starting point of a transition is not the outcome but the ending you and your employees have to make to leave the old situation behind."

Start at the Ending

When a CEO announces a tactical shift like a refocus on growth, Bridges says leaders need to be mindful that people are being told to let go of the world they are familiar with. Even if this appears less traumatic than the announcement of layoffs, Bridges says the change will still demand an important psychological transition that may be met with resistance.

"If you want real change, you are asking people to let go of some of the guidelines and rules they are now using," says Bridges. "You are saying that what used to be rewarded is now going to be dysfunctional. You may be telling people to let go of 'playing it safe and covering your ass'—and that's scary if that's the behavior that was getting rewarded. For instance, managers with cost-cutting skills may not be as valuable now as innovators who can move quickly."

Leaders have important communication jobs at this stage, Bridges says. First, "start selling the problem"— talk in every forum possible about the reasons for change and the cost of not addressing the problem. One useful tool: put together a one-minute speech about what the change is and why it is necessary. Not only will this clarify the issue in your mind, but it will also ensure consistency as the speech is given again and again.

Next, leaders have to focus employees on defining what to let go of. A leader who can't do this, says Bridges, "is a leader who later finds people haven't really let go of the past and are stuck in the middle of transition long after they should have made a new beginning."

In this stage, leaders can communicate more by actions than by words. Allocating space or money in a new and public way, reassigning a leader who has been ambivalent about a change, or putting on a ceremony or celebratory event can help dramatize an ending, he says.

And don't overreact to resistance or questions: expect to give the same information over and over.

"Remember that during endings, people crave information although, ironically, they are sometimes distracted and may ask several times," says Bridges. Also keep in mind that this is when people are learning to let go of things that are going to go away and are shifting their attention. It takes a surprising amount of energy.

Navigate the Neutral Zone

"The neutral zone—that halfway time between the old way of doing things and the new—can be the most difficult time because there's no solid ground. Employees are asking, 'You've said the old way doesn't work, so what does?'" says Bridges.

For example, in a company launching growth strategies, leaders can't yet prove their tactics will work, identify which investments will pay off, or define exactly what jobs need to be realigned or changed. There may be multiple projects launched, sending mixed signals about plans going forward.

"This is when people don't know the rules because the rules are up for grabs," says Bridges.

The good news is that the neutral zone can also provide conditions for trying new things. Here, Bridges says,

> **Talk in every forum possible about the reasons for change and the cost of not addressing the problem.**

it is key for leaders to show that they themselves are willing to try some risks and ask themselves and employees often if "there are other things to get things done."

"This is a different kind of communication than 'Just do your job' or 'Let's be more creative,'" says Bridges. "This is the time for a consistent, well-integrated conversation about 'How we're going to get this work done.' This has to do with organizational arrangements, but the strategy will live or die on this."

Bridges believes many managers flounder in this period, in part because they are "too many levels up and don't know the nuts and bolts of how the work gets done."

"When you read narrative accounts of people who are successful in big transitions, they are on the floor a lot," says Bridges. "This is the time to help people get more control of their situations, understand what is happening to them, and feel supported."

This is also time to clarify new priorities and reinforce

them with examples and rewards. And set short-range goals for people to aim toward. "Now is a time when people get discouraged easily, because it can seem that nothing important is happening," says Bridges. "It's crucial to give people a sense of achievement and of movement, even if you have to stretch the point a bit."

Launch a New Beginning

"You need to remember that as a leader, you are much further into the new beginning than your followers are," says Bridges. "You've known about the change longer, you see the bigger picture, you are more familiar with alternatives, and your identity may not be as tied to the old way of doing things as theirs is."

That means that leaders need to be consistent in their messages and watch the way their words and actions match up, Bridges says. Reinforcing the changes is key: Don't preach teamwork and then publicly praise individual contribution. Don't preach risk taking and then reward no mistakes. And don't preach feedback and then punish those who speak up.

Keep in mind also that people throughout the organization don't have the same pace and style for absorbing changes. "Transition is a ragged process," says Bridges.

That's why leaders continue to talk about the purpose behind the planned change and the picture of how the outcome will look and feel. They also keep describing the step-by-step plan for phasing in the outcome for employees.

Successful leaders don't forget to communicate on the individual level, says Bridges, and focus on talking about the part each employee will play in the outcome. Until this information is provided, many people will feel left out and find it difficult to make a new beginning, he says.

Bridges suggests that leaders set up transition management teams to keep communication flowing and give people new insight into the problems being faced by the company as it comes out of the neutral zone and redefines itself.

"When people play a part in something like a transition management team, they are tacitly at least implicated in the outcome—they accept and are committed to the change," says Bridges. "In most cases, excellence is about seven parts commitment and three parts strategy."

Reprint C0404B

Debriefing Howard Gardner

Tactics for Changing Minds

• • •

Lauren Keller Johnson

You've got an exciting new idea that you feel certain will generate huge company benefits. Perhaps it's a break-through product line or an innovative way to improve performance. The advantages of your idea are crystal clear, but when you present it to direct reports, peers, and superiors, you meet with resistance. Some people question its potential. Others express concerns about the costs or time involved. Still others initially seem intrigued by your proposal but fail to do anything with it afterward. You wonder how you'll garner the coordinated teamwork required to put your idea into action.

As Howard Gardner, author of *Changing Minds: The Art and Science of Changing Our Own and Other People's Minds,* explains, we find it increasingly difficult to open ourselves up to new ideas as we age. Our worldviews ossify, making us less inclined to consider something radically different. Resistance intensifies if we experience unpleasantness after embracing a new idea. For instance, a previous attempt to adopt a new customer service strategy fails, so managers and employees shy away from similar proposals later. For these reasons, leaders seeking support for their ideas can't rely on a single method of persuasion; they need to employ tactics carefully tailored to affect disparate people.

Say It Often and in Many Ways

In *Changing Minds,* Gardner introduces seven levers for breaking through resistance to new ideas. Some of these levers—such as providing convincing data and earning listeners' trust—are familiar to most persuaders. But several seem far less intuitive, even to seasoned communicators. In particular, Gardner says, "many people mistakenly assume that delivering their message just once will make them convincing." Yet no matter how good your idea or compelling your presentation is, "you need to send your message many times to reinforce it in your listeners' minds."

Thus Gardner advocates what he calls *representational redescriptions*—delivering your proposal in a variety of formats. Such formats may include engaging stories, startling numerical information, graphic depictions such as charts or cartoons, humor, demonstrations and simulations, vivid descriptions of enticing or disturbing scenarios, and, most important, embodying the message in your own behavior. By delivering your message through a mix of formats, Gardner maintains, "you increase the chances that your audience will understand your idea." And the deeper your listeners' understanding, the greater their ability to let go of firmly entrenched notions and embrace new ones.

Using representational redescriptions may seem straightforward. But to get the most from them, managers must apply them artfully.

Lead to a Familiar Problem

Imagine that you've just attended a conference where you learned of an intriguing new technology that many organizations in your industry have adopted. You believe that, to remain competitive, your company needs to adopt the technology. You also know that this initiative would be costly at first, so you anticipate significant

Seven Levers for Changing Minds

In *Changing Minds,* Howard Gardner discusses seven levers for persuading others to embrace new ideas:

1. **Reason:** You present all relevant considerations of an idea, including its pros and cons.
2. **Research:** You provide numerical and other information about your idea's ramifications, or data relevant to your idea.
3. **Resonance:** You and your ideas are convincing to your listener because of your track record, effective presentation, and sense of your audience.
4. **Representational redescriptions:** You deliver your message in a variety of formats, including stories, statistics, and graphics.
5. **Resources and rewards:** You draw on resources to demonstrate the value of your idea and provide incentives to adopt your idea.
6. **Real-world events:** You monitor events in the world on a daily basis and, whenever possible, draw on them to support your idea.
7. **Resistances:** You devote considerable energy to identifying the principal resistances to your ideas (both conscious and unconscious resistances) and try to defuse them directly and implicitly.

resistance. How might you use representational re-descriptions to persuade managers in your organization to consider the technology?

Gardner advises against simply cobbling together a blend of statistics, stories, and other formats. Instead, frame your mix of message formats in neutral terms that help your audience ease into evaluating a legitimate, familiar problem objectively. For instance, say something like, "Remember how we lost those three customers last quarter because of order-processing errors? I have some insights about how that may have happened." Then tell the story of what went wrong.

This narrative structure, Gardner says, is far more effective than starting off with a description of how you attended the conference and what you learned there—which is akin to saying, "I know something you don't know."

Leverage the Power of Contrast

Contrasting scenarios can also prove powerfully convincing. Returning to the conference example, Gardner says, you might ask your audience to identify the company's current beliefs about major change. Perhaps managers and employees tend to favor the status quo, owing to previous disasters that came with implementation of large-scale change. Are people in effect telling themselves and one another in subtle ways, "We should avoid flash-in-the-pan solutions to our problems"?

Now challenge your listeners to imagine new beliefs that contrast sharply with the existing views. Such devil's advocate responses might include "This new technology is the wave of the future," "We'll be out of business if we don't stay current," or "We need to do whatever it takes to stay ahead of our competitors."

By inviting audience members to create this sense of contrast themselves, you help them move from old beliefs to new ones.

Know Audience Intelligence

In *Changing Minds,* Gardner describes the numerous ways in which human intelligence manifests itself. These include linguistic intelligence (having a strong facility with spoken and written language), logical-mathematical intelligence (understanding causal relationships and numerical information), spatial intelligence (forming and manipulating spatial representations in one's mind), bodily-kinesthetic intelligence (solving problems using whole body or fine motor skills), and interpersonal intelligence (working effectively with and influencing others).

To select the right blend of representational redescriptions to employ, seek to discern the types of intelligence characterizing your intended audience members. This takes keen observation. Ask yourself: Who seems to understand customers' needs best? Who learns most by reading about or discussing new ideas? Who appears highly responsive to factual and numerical information? Who can't resist playing with product demonstrations?

You can also learn more about your audience's intelligence through informal focus groups. Ask participants how they prefer to solve problems and learn. Invite them to describe incidents in which they didn't understand a new idea that someone else presented—and to explain why the communication failed.

"You can learn a lot from things that didn't work with a particular person or audience," Gardner says.

Then adapt your delivery accordingly. For example, suppose you're advocating a new customer service initiative, and some audience members excel at interpersonal intelligence. In this case, you might challenge your listeners to define key customers' attitudes toward your company—to help them begin seeing the urgent need for the initiative. For bodily-kinesthetically intelligent audience members, invite them to put themselves in the place of product end users, so they can experience user-interface problems firsthand. For people with strong logical-mathematical intelligence, lay out the consequences of not implementing the initiative. Compare that dire scenario with the rosier reality—including hard-core profitability numbers—that could be had if the company improved its customer service.

Draw on Your Resources

None of us is equally comfortable with or skilled at all the representational redescription formats available for communicating ideas. Get help with those formats in which you're weakest. For instance, Gardner recommends asking a colleague who is especially good at storytelling to present your idea at a department or team meeting. Ask another who's a strong writer to craft an article for the company newsletter.

Your goal? To present that promising idea with enough frequency and variety that others will understand it, remember it, and—most important—embrace it.

Reprint U0406D

Communication as a Change Tool

• • •

Stever Robbins

Tim Wallace knew he had a problem: customers were complaining about the delivery of built-to-order products and unhappy with his staff's lack of response. He knew a major change was needed but wasn't sure whether to start writing just another angry memo.

So Wallace decided instead to ask an unhappy customer to be videotaped, describing his experience with the company and his frustrations in asking for changes. The 15-minute video was eventually screened for 400 plant employees in a series of small meetings.

"A few mouths actually droppped open," Wallace recounts. "A minority was defensive. But just as many were saying, 'We've got to do something about this. We've got to do something.'"

Wallace's videotape became a catalyst that focused plant workers and managers on a problem that no one had been able to "get off the dime" to solve for years, he says. But the tape also was a classic illustration of the importance of communication in a change initiative, a key component experts say is often overlooked when leaders attempt to transform an organization.

"Change and communication go hand in hand," says Dan S. Cohen, who, with coauthor John P. Kotter, collected the stories of Wallace and other successful change leaders for the book *The Heart of Change*. "Yet too often I've heard leaders complain, 'I *said* this is what we're doing,' but then it still isn't happening.

"In the end, it's that communication and emotion"— the ability of employees to respond on a personal level— "that sustains the urgency to change. And it has to be recharged, again and again. Change isn't a 50-yard race, it's a marathon."

Cohen and other experts say that communicating this need and urgency is crucial for getting people behind a proposed change. Directives and memos from the top aren't enough: clear messages backed with concrete examples are needed for employees to focus and put their energies behind a new effort. The right messengers need to be on the front lines, reinforcing the ideas and providing the key link in the feedback loop. Most change efforts convey information about the desired change, but that's where most communication stops. Executives who want to make a lasting change in an organization need to have an ongoing conversation with the people who can tell them what is—and isn't—working every day.

Information Made Visible

"Organizations have complex, well-developed immune systems, aimed at preserving the status quo," write Peter Senge et al. in *The Dance of Change.* So leaders who want to launch a change initiative that will last have to first understand "how significant change invariably starts locally and how it grows over time," they say.

That's why showing small groups of employees the videotape of an unhappy customer complaining about faulty products and services has a far greater effect than a memo from the CEO outlining the need for "better customer relations." Not only did employees get an up-close look at the impact of the failure to remedy the situation, they were then immediately able to start talking about their own ideas regarding changes they could make to address the problem.

Similarly, Senge et al. cite the story of a nationwide plant maintenance initiative that was launched by a chemical company with great fanfare, only to sputter out after initially strong results. The management team had celebrated the success of its pilot program with a party and, confident that others in the company would want to learn from the experience, produced a booklet that described the new strategy. Yet even after the pilot was expanded to several other plants, the program failed once the first trainees moved on.

The team then regrouped and chose to narrow its focus. They zeroed in on pumps, which are trouble-prone yet crucial to overall production efficiency. They then further isolated their ten worst pumps. This focused effort grew to include 13 different locations. Although some plants still rejected the change, the programs that did take hold emboldened the management team to expand the effort to address larger maintenance challenges and overall plant operations. Starting with a smaller picture of change, the team concluded, was better.

In yet another example, Cohen and Kotter describe a purchasing manager who was trying to cut costs, without much success. So he quietly assembled an exhibit of work gloves, all purchased at wildly different prices from different vendors by his managers around the country. He piled the gloves on a table—revealing a *lot* of duplication—and invited his managers in for a visit. They quickly understood the problem.

These "visualizations," as Cohen and Kotter call them, provide the kind of dramatic confrontation with the facts that can convince employees of the need for change and remove some of the emotional blocks that reinforce the status quo.

A Pivotal Management Role

In his book *Real Change Leaders,* Jon R. Katzenbach writes that a frequently overlooked position on the organizational chart—the middle manager—can be crucial to a change initiative. Katzenbach says middle managers play such an important role because they are the ones who are directly responsible for improving performance through people.

These managers are the most plugged in to the concerns of employees and are the ones who will demonstrate daily the company's belief in the change effort. Without that kind of demonstration, cynical employees can easily shrug off the latest pronouncement from the CEO's office. Ignoring change directives became such an art at one manufacturer that employees even used the acronym AFP—"Another Fine Program"—for describing change initiatives.

"Too many leaders don't think through the implications, all the way down the line," says Cohen. "So when you and I hear about the change for the first time at some company announcement, there is no one to ask, 'What does this mean to me and my job?' In that sense, is the CEO really the most credible?"

Middle managers are key in communicating change because they are the people employees look to first to see if there is real acceptance of the idea, says Cohen. "Too many leaders don't realize that without the middle manager behind it, too many people think, 'I don't have to change. It's not going to happen anyway,'" says Cohen. "Too often the next level down says, 'Just let it go. If my boss doesn't tell me it is important, then it won't happen.'"

Because middle managers occupy such a central role, breaking down the communication plan to target them first in small sessions should be one of the cornerstones of a change initiative. But be prepared: middle managers, knowing they will hear the complaints and concerns of their unit employees, will be eager to ask questions and get details about job definitions, restructuring, compensation, and new policies.

Creating a Feedback Loop

Don't forget that communication should be a two-way street from the moment a change initiative is announced. When people help design new processes, they will be much more likely to use them. The more people contribute to answering the "how" questions, the more they will buy into making the "how" work.

In an aircraft company that Cohen surveyed, a new CEO was certain that he needed to quickly and definitively change how production problems were being handled. For senior management, he outlined the problem and what needed to happen in meetings.

But in order to reach frontline employees, the new

> Communication should be a two-way street from the moment a change initiative is announced.

leader spent time walking around the plant to talk to employees on the job. Instead of calling them to an auditorium, he found out where groups hung out, such as in the "smoking pit." He usually started by asking workers about the company and the problems they faced, and then he would ask for advice about the production problems that threatened to shut down the plant.

The weekly tour created a kind of automatic feedback program: when new ideas and steps were implemented, the CEO would be back within a few days to talk to workers about the changes, their reactions, and their suggestions for fine-tuning the process.

In another company, the CEO set up a weekly reporting program, where unit heads could collect questions and problems that the change initiative was running into. According to Cohen, this allowed him to use companywide meetings to confront the issues head on and measure what kind of misinformation was flowing around the change.

As positive change begins to emerge, it's just as important to remember that the feedback loop can also be a good way to celebrate successes, both large and small. If people don't notice the difference, point it out. Choose high-profile decisions that send a message throughout the organization. The more the new ways contrast with the old, the stronger that message will be.

For Further Reading

Real Change Leaders by Jon R. Katzenbach and the RCL Team (1997, Three Rivers Press).

The Heart of Change: Real-Life Stories of How People Change Their Organizations by John P. Kotter and Dan S. Cohen (2002, Harvard Business School Press).

The Dance of Change: The Challenges to Sustaining Momentum in Learning Organizations by Peter Senge et al. (1999, Currency Doubleday). ´

Reprint C0207C

About the Contributors

Katherine Kane is a contributor to Harvard Management Mentor.

Tom Krattenmaker is a Philadelphia-area author and the director of news and information at Swarthmore College.

Robert S. Kaplan is the Marvin Bower Professor of Leadership Development at Harvard Business School and Chairman of the Balanced Scorecard Collaborative.

David P. Norton is Co-founder and President of the Balanced Scorecard Collaborative.

Lauren Keller Johnson is a contributor to *Harvard Management Update*.

Nick Morgan is former editor of *Harvard Management Communication Letter*.

Sharon Drew Morgen is an Austin, Tex.–based consultant who works with companies and employees to improve change processes and decision making.

Lila Booth is a contributor to *Harvard Management Update*.

Loren Gary is editor of Newsletters at HBS Publishing.

Betty A. Marton is a contributor to *Harvard Management Update*.

About the Contributors

Rebecca M. Sanders is a contributor to *Harvard Management Update*.

Angelia Herrin is group editor of HBS Publishing Newsletters and Conferences.

Stever Robbins is president of VentureCoach, Inc., a Cambridge, Mass.-based executive coaching firm.

Harvard Business Review Paperback Series

The Harvard Business Review Paperback Series offers the best thinking on cutting-edge management ideas from the world's leading thinkers, researchers, and managers. Designed for leaders who believe in the power of ideas to change business, these books will be useful to managers at all levels of experience, but especially senior executives and general managers. In addition, this series is widely used in training and executive development programs.

Books are priced at $19.95 U.S.
Price subject to change.

Title	Product #
Harvard Business Review **Interviews with CEOs**	3294
Harvard Business Review on **Advances in Strategy**	8032
Harvard Business Review on **Appraising Employee Performance**	7685
Harvard Business Review on **Becoming a High Performance Manager**	1296
Harvard Business Review on **Brand Management**	1445
Harvard Business Review on **Breakthrough Leadership**	8059
Harvard Business Review on **Breakthrough Thinking**	181X
Harvard Business Review on **Building Personal and Organizational Resilience**	2721
Harvard Business Review on **Business and the Environment**	2336
Harvard Business Review on **Change**	8842
Harvard Business Review on **Compensation**	701X
Harvard Business Review on **Corporate Ethics**	273X
Harvard Business Review on **Corporate Governance**	2379
Harvard Business Review on **Corporate Responsibility**	2748
Harvard Business Review on **Corporate Strategy**	1429
Harvard Business Review on **Crisis Management**	2352
Harvard Business Review on **Culture and Change**	8369
Harvard Business Review on **Customer Relationship Management**	6994
Harvard Business Review on **Decision Making**	5572

To order, call 1-800-668-6780, or go online at www.HBSPress.org

Title	Product #
Harvard Business Review on **Doing Business in China**	6387
Harvard Business Review on **Effective Communication**	1437
Harvard Business Review on **Entrepreneurship**	9105
Harvard Business Review on **Finding and Keeping the Best People**	5564
Harvard Business Review on **Innovation**	6145
Harvard Business Review on **Knowledge Management**	8818
Harvard Business Review on **Leadership**	8834
Harvard Business Review on **Leadership at the Top**	2756
Harvard Business Review on **Leadership in a Changed World**	5011
Harvard Business Review on **Leading in Turbulent Times**	1806
Harvard Business Review on **Managing Diversity**	7001
Harvard Business Review on **Managing High-Tech Industries**	1828
Harvard Business Review on **Managing People**	9075
Harvard Business Review on **Managing Projects**	6395
Harvard Business Review on **Managing the Value Chain**	2344
Harvard Business Review on **Managing Uncertainty**	9083
Harvard Business Review on **Managing Your Career**	1318
Harvard Business Review on **Marketing**	8040
Harvard Business Review on **Measuring Corporate Performance**	8826
Harvard Business Review on **Mergers and Acquisitions**	5556
Harvard Business Review on **The Mind of the Leader**	6409
Harvard Business Review on **Motivating People**	1326
Harvard Business Review on **Negotiation**	2360
Harvard Business Review on **Nonprofits**	9091
Harvard Business Review on **Organizational Learning**	6153
Harvard Business Review on **Strategic Alliances**	1334
Harvard Business Review on **Strategies for Growth**	8850
Harvard Business Review on **The Business Value of IT**	9121
Harvard Business Review on **The Innovative Enterprise**	130X
Harvard Business Review on **Turnarounds**	6366
Harvard Business Review on **What Makes a Leader**	6374
Harvard Business Review on **Work and Life Balance**	3286

Management Dilemmas: Case Studies from the Pages of Harvard Business Review

How often do you wish you could turn to a panel of experts to guide you through tough management situations? The Management Dilemmas series provides just that. Drawn from the pages of *Harvard Business Review*, each insightful volume poses several perplexing predicaments and shares the problem-solving wisdom of leading experts. Engagingly written, these solutions-oriented collections help managers make sound judgment calls when addressing everyday management dilemmas.

These books are priced at $19.95 U.S.
Price subject to change.

Title	Product #
Management Dilemmas: **When Change Comes Undone**	5038
Management Dilemmas: **When Good People Behave Badly**	5046
Management Dilemmas: **When Marketing Becomes a Minefield**	290X
Management Dilemmas: **When People Are the Problem**	7138
Management Dilemmas: **When Your Strategy Stalls**	712X

Harvard Business Essentials

In the fast-paced world of business today, everyone needs a personal resource—a place to go for advice, coaching, background information, or answers. The Harvard Business Essentials series fits the bill. Concise and straightforward, these books provide highly practical advice for readers at all levels of experience. Whether you are a new manager interested in expanding your skills or an experienced executive looking to stay on top, these solution-oriented books give you the reliable tips and tools you need to improve your performance and get the job done. Harvard Business Essentials titles will quickly become your constant companions and trusted guides.

These books are priced at $19.95 U.S., except as noted.
Price subject to change.

Title	Product #
Harvard Business Essentials: **Negotiation**	1113
Harvard Business Essentials: **Managing Creativity and Innovation**	1121
Harvard Business Essentials: **Managing Change and Transition**	8741
Harvard Business Essentials: **Hiring and Keeping the Best People**	875X
Harvard Business Essentials: **Finance for Managers**	8768
Harvard Business Essentials: **Business Communication**	113X
Harvard Business Essentials: **Manager's Toolkit ($24.95)**	2896
Harvard Business Essentials: **Managing Projects Large and Small**	3213
Harvard Business Essentials: **Creating Teams with an Edge**	290X
Harvard Business Essentials: **Entrepreneur's Toolkit**	4368
Harvard Business Essentials: **Coaching and Mentoring**	435X
Harvard Business Essentials: **Crisis Management**	4376

The Results-Driven Manager

The Results-Driven Manager series collects timely articles from *Harvard Management Update* and *Harvard Management Communication Letter* to help senior to middle managers sharpen their skills, increase their effectiveness, and gain a competitive edge. Presented in a concise, accessible format to save managers valuable time, these books offer authoritative insights and techniques for improving job performance and achieving immediate results.

These books are priced at $14.95 U.S.
Price subject to change.

Title	Product #
The Results-Driven Manager:	
Face-to-Face Communications for Clarity and Impact	3477
The Results-Driven Manager:	
Managing Yourself for the Career You Want	3469
The Results-Driven Manager:	
Presentations That Persuade and Motivate	3493
The Results-Driven Manager: **Teams That Click**	3507
The Results-Driven Manager:	
Winning Negotiations That Preserve Relationships	3485
The Results-Driven Manager: **Dealing with Difficult People**	6344
The Results-Driven Manager: **Taking Control of Your Time**	6352
The Results-Driven Manager: **Getting People on Board**	6360
The Results-Driven Manager:	
Motivating People for Improved Performance	7790
The Results-Driven Manager: **Becoming an Effective Leader**	7804
The Results-Driven Manager:	
Managing Change to Reduce Resistance	7812

How to Order

Harvard Business School Press publications are available worldwide
from your local bookseller or online retailer.
You can also call

1-800-668-6780

Our product consultants are available to help you
8:00 a.m.–6:00 p.m., Monday–Friday, Eastern Time.
Outside the U.S. and Canada, call: 617-783-7450
Please call about special discounts for quantities greater than ten.

You can order online at

www.HBSPress.org